Contradict Capitalism

An Introduction to Marxist Economics

Lenny Flank

Red and Black Publishers, St Petersburg, Florida, 2007

Publishers Cataloging in Publication Data –
Flank, Lenny
  Contradictions of Capitalism: An Introduction to Marxist Economics/Lenny Flank
  p. cm.
   ISBN: 978-0-9791813-9-9
1.Communism. 2. Economics.
I. Title
HB501 .F53 2007
335.4   LCCN: 2007932143

Red and Black Publishers, PO Box 7542, St Petersburg, Florida, 33734
Contact us at: info@RedandBlackPublishers.com

       Printed and manufactured in the United States of America

Contents

Introduction

In the latter half of the nineteenth century, Karl Marx set forth, in a series of writings, a critical analysis of the economic mode of production then being established throughout Europe and North America, the mode of production known as capitalism. Marx concluded that the inherent contradictions and crises produced within the capitalist system would doom it to eventual collapse, and would result in its replacement by the socialist mode of production.

In the early years of the twentieth century, a number of people led by the German socialist Eduard Bernstein set out to modify or revise Marx's analysis, and concluded that, contrary to Marx's assertions, there were no inherent weaknesses in capitalism that would eventually destroy it. Socialism, according to the revisionists, could only result from a process of economic reform and political organization.

In 1917, Marxian economic analysis was clouded even further by the Bolshevik Revolution in Russia. The Leninists, like the revisionists, used and abused Marxist theory for their own ends. Marx himself, commenting on the widespread distortion and misunderstanding of his thought, remarked shortly before his death, "I am not a Marxist."

This confusion is not at all helped by Marx's ponderous and pedantic style of writing. The average reader would find it a monumental task to plow through the thousands of pages written by Marx.

In addition, since Marx's death in the late 19th century, the capitalist system which he was studying has undergone profound changes. In some cases, Marx had noted the beginnings of these trends and commented on them briefly, but it remains for modern Marxists to continue to apply the Marxian method of analysis to our world. In particular, the development of the modern monopoly corporate society and the rise and fall of the non-market "Leninist" states are economic phenomena which cry out for a Marxist investigation and analysis.

This book, then, is an attempt to begin an investigation of modern political economy using the Marxian method of analysis. It presents a comprehensive study of the development of capitalism, from its beginnings in the feudalist society to its modern corporate incarnation. And, since developments in the capitalist economies are inextricably linked with developments in the non-industrialized "Third World" and the non-market "Leninist" states, these phenomena are also examined.

A word of definition may be needed here. Throughout this work, "Leninism" is used to refer to that socio-politico-economic system introduced by Lenin in 1917 and more or less copied by others. While they are known under various names— Leninism, Stalinism, Trotskyism, Maoism, Titoism, Castroism—each of these "Marxist-Leninist" regimes are essentially the same in their basic structure, and are produced by similar socio-economic circumstances. For this reason, I refer to them collectively as "Leninist" modes of production, to distinguish them from the communist system discussed by Marx.

This work can only be an introduction to Marxian economic theory. The reader who wishes to pursue a more detailed investigation is referred to the voluminous writings of Marx, in particular the three volumes of *Capital*. More recent analyses can be found in the works of authorities who have applied the Marxian method to modern economics. Prominent among these are Mandel, Baran, Magdoff and Sweezy.

Our economic analysis of capitalism must begin at the beginning. Therefore, we will begin our investigation with the historical progenitor of capitalism—the feudalist mode of production.

ONE: Feudal Mode of Production

The feudal system reigned supreme in Europe from approximately the fall of the Roman Empire to the mid-18th century. Unlike our industrialized corporate system, feudalism was primarily agricultural, and was particularly well-suited for bringing large tracts of land under cultivation.

The feudalist political system is best described as one of hierarchy. Each feudal lord had his subordinates who owed him unquestioning loyalty, and his superiors in the hierarchy to whom he himself owed absolute fealty. Thus, the feudal king received the loyalty and support of the various barons, dukes and other nobility, who in turn received loyalty and support from the various fiefdoms within their realm.

The fief was the basic social and economic unit of the feudalist system. These were areas of land which had been set aside for the exclusive use of a particular feudal lord. The political administration of this system was carried out by an individual king, who was one of the large landowners, or by a state bureaucracy run by a consortium of the major landowning families. The barons and other nobility received their fiefs from this political apparatus, usually in reward for some service rendered or for exemplary loyalty. Within their realms, the word of the nobility was literally law. The feudal lord had complete authority to decree laws, mint coins and impose taxes.

It is important to note that the feudal fief was not the lord's personal property—he did not "own" it. Fiefdom is more correctly to be viewed as a right of occupation and use. The feudal noble could not purchase a fief, although he could sometimes inherit one from his predecessor under the right of primogeniture.

The feudal economy was almost exclusively based upon agriculture, and the population was divided into two basic economic groups. The apex of the social system was the feudal nobility who controlled fiefs. The large majority of people were serfs or peasant laborers. They owned no land and controlled no fiefs; instead, they produced their means of living by working the land held by the feudal landlords. In exchange for their right to work this land, serfs were obligated to turn over some portion of their output to the feudal lord. In some instances, these taxes took the form of a fixed amount of output, i.e., so many bushels of wheat, so many pounds of vegetables. In other cases, the serf was obligated to work a certain amount of time in the lord's fields. For instance, the serf might be compelled to work three days a week in the lord's fields, allowing four days to work his own lands.

Thus, the life of a serf was a dull routine of working the fields for long hours to produce enough to pay his feudal taxes and have enough left over to feed himself and his family. When the nobility needed more resources, feudal taxes went up and the serf worked harder for less. When the fiefdom was involved in war, it was the serf who was conscripted and who bore the brunt of the fighting.

It is easy to see the economic basis of the feudal system. The serfs, working in the fields, produce nearly all of the economy's wealth. The feudal lord, by contrast, performs no work and produces no wealth, but, by virtue of his control over the land, he can compel his serfs to produce more than they themselves will consume. This surplus production is then appropriated by the feudal lord in the form of taxes.

This naked process of exploitation could—and did— produce rebellious feelings on the part of the serfs, and continuous peasant uprisings and rebellions are a prominent feature of feudal history. In order to justify their privileged position and to placate the rebellious population, the feudal aristocracy turned to political and religious thought. In nearly all feudal landowning systems, the titular head of state, whether an individual monarch (as the European King) or the executive of a collective bureaucracy (as the Japanese Emperor), was viewed as a divine god-king who ruled by religious right.

Thus, religious piety was used to justify the exploitation of the serfs by the aristocracy. The hierarchy inherent in the structures of Church and State, this ethos taught, reflected the will of God. The place each person occupied in the social hierarchy was a manifestation of Divine Will, and therefore the task of humanity was to quietly assume a God-given role and please God through devotion and loyalty to the higher levels of the social structure. These superiors, the Church concluded, ruled by Divine Right, and thus to rebel against the legitimate authority of the King and the nobility was not only a political crime, but a sin against God's established order.

It is important to keep in mind the enormous political and economic power wielded by the organized church in the feudal period. In many instances, the feudal lord who controlled a serf's fief was an abbot, bishop or other Church official. In a society where religious authority intermingled with the secular, the threat of excommunication was something not to be taken lightly, and the charge of heresy was a virtual death sentence.

It is obvious, however, that the politico-religious structure of feudalism was merely a justification for, and a method of safeguarding, the appropriation of economic wealth from the peasantry by the nobility. The beneficiaries of the feudal economic system—the aristocracy and the Church—utilized their political, military and religious powers to protect this exploitative economic relationship. As feudal society developed, however, a new economic class was arising within it that would eventually undermine and destroy feudalism.

TWO: The Rise of Capitalism

The eventual downfall of the feudalist system can ultimately be traced to the growth of the towns. While the agrarian basis of the feudal economy tied most people to the landed fiefs, there were in many areas small towns and ports which served as trading posts. Through trade with neighboring kingdoms, these commercial centers became small colonies of merchants and artisans, who produced and traded tools, weapons, armor and other implements.

A natural division of labor thus arose, with the urban artisans producing manufactured implements and imported goods, while the rural fiefdoms produced food and agricultural products. At first, trade took place only when both parties possessed a surplus over what they needed for themselves. Eventually, however, urban artisans began more and more to produce implements specifically for trade, and began to obtain their own necessities solely through this trade. These articles, produced for exchange rather than for the immediate use of the person who produced them, mark the beginning of the "commodity" economy.

Since feudal taxes are paid "in kind", that is, as a direct portion of the serf's agricultural output, there is little need for a monetary system in the fief. As commodity trade between the fiefs and the urban areas increases, however, the need for money as a medium of exchange becomes apparent. Under the direct barter of commodities, commodity exchangers have to keep looking until they find a partner who is willing to trade the commodity desired. Using money, commodities can be exchanged at any time for a cash equivalent, and this cash can then be used to trade for the desired item.

Thus, each fiefdom took to minting coins for use in exchange. The use of gold and silver as money is not due to any mysterious qualities in the metals themselves —clamshells or cattle would do just as well as a medium of exchange. Coins were made of gold and silver simply because these metals were nonperishable and were simple to carry, mint and divide into subunits.

This monetarization of the feudal economy, however, forced profound changes in the socio-economic structures of feudalism. The feudal lords, who needed the weapons, armor and manufactured goods produced by the urban artisans, also needed the money to exchange for them. As a result, the feudal convention of a "tax in kind" was modified, and feudal lords turned to monetary taxes and monetary fees —"rent" —in addition to the agricultural tax. As the use of money became more and more widespread, the portion of the economy that was engaged in commodity exchange rather than in agrarian production increased.

This growing counter-economy presented a mortal danger to the aristocracy by undermining the very basis of its economic privilege. As a result, the feudal nobility attacked it, and the ideo-religious ethos of the Church was turned to the task of limiting the growing commodity economy. Priests now spoke of the sins of "avarice" and "usury". The Church declared it a sin to lend money at interest, and exhorted the faithful to abandon the sinful world of monetary and material interests. *"Homo mercator vix aut numquam Deo placere potesti,"* the Church warned. "A person of commerce can rarely or never be pleasing to God."

While recognizing the threat that the growing merchant class (or bourgeoisie —"town dwellers" —as they were known) represented, the feudal aristocracy at the same time was forced to concede that they could not live without the merchants. Trade with the artisans provided weapons, armor and such exotic imported goods as Chinese silk and porcelain, Indian tea and spices, and Arab foods and technology. These things were beyond the reach of the feudal nobles, and they were absolutely dependent upon the bourgeoisie to obtain them.

As this system of trade grew, a transition began to take place in the methods of commodity production. Now, instead of merely importing exotic commodities which were then exchanged through the monetary system, merchants with sufficient monetary resources began the direct manufacture of commodities for resale at a profit, thereby increasing the amount of money available to them for new production. Under this system, money no longer served exclusively as a medium of exchange—it could be directly utilized to produce still more money. This process marked the introduction of "capital" by the infant bourgeoisie.

As the merchant class grew in size and influence, so too did the urban areas, known as burghs, where they set up shop. As these commercial centers began to expand their trade ties across Europe, however, they ran head-on into the hodge-podge of fiefs which quilted the countryside, each controlled by a particular feudal lord and each having its own system of laws, tolls, taxes and legal tender. To overcome this stifling maze of regulation and taxation, the bourgeoisie raised the banner of nationalism, and called for the control of each national area by a single feudal ruler, with a unified system of law, taxes and currency.

Since the feudal nobles were always anxious to expand their fiefs at the expense of their neighbors, nationalist ideas found ready allies in both the bourgeoisie and the nobility. In each national area, a single feudal noble gradually expanded his power until he had imposed his rule upon the entire nation. This "monarch" was in turn allied with and supported by the bourgeoisie, upon which he depended for the cash he needed to buy weapons and hire soldiers for his wars of consolidation.

As the need to defend the monarchy from the predations of other feudal rulers grew, so did the king's need for cash. The merchants, for their part, were in constant need of new sources of exotic commodities for trade. Once again, the monarchies and the merchants found their interests to be mutual. The monarchs of Europe commissioned overseas expeditions of exploration and conquest—Drake, Vespucci, Columbus, Cabot and Magellan. These expeditions resulted in overseas colonies that were kept under the economic and political control of the monarchy. This "mercantilist" system provided the fledgling bourgeoisie with new sources of exotic trade commodities, and the taxes and tribute collected in the colonies increased the coffers of the feudal monarchy.

The need for cash also led the feudal nobles to divert parts of their traditional fiefs from food production to the raising of sheep for wool and other profitable commodities. This in turn forced large numbers of peasant farmers and serfs off of the land and out of the feudal fiefs. Penniless and starving, these paupers crowded into the towns and burghs, where they had nothing left to sell for their living except their own ability to perform labor. They were hired by the artisans and merchants as laborers to produce commodities for trade, and thus formed the beginnings of the proletariat or working class.

By the time of the 18th century, the twin frameworks of feudalist monarchy and bourgeois commodity production existed side by side in most of Europe. These two systems were, however, entirely incompatible. Feudal monarchy required a heavily agricultural economy in which wealth could be directly appropriated from serf labor. It also required a rigid hierarchy of authority, supported by the ideals of unquestioning loyalty and obedience. It required strong economic and legal ties to keep the serfs on the fief where their labor could be exploited, and it also required that the major source of wealth in the economy be the land, over which the aristocracy had complete control.

The rising capitalist system, by contrast, required a commercial and manufacturing economy. The aristocratic privileges of the feudal nobility were in conflict with the merchant class's need for freedom of economic action. The merchants also required methods of removing the landless serfs from the fiefs and turning them into propertyless industrial laborers.

By the middle of the 18th century, the conflict between the two social systems came to a head. With the capitalist class steadily undermining the basis of the feudal system, it was a battle which the monarchy could not hope to win. In 1775, the explosion began in what was then an obscure and distant British colony in North America. Under the banner of the merchants, the North American colonists attacked the feudal institutions of monarchy and Divine Right, and established the first state dedicated to the bourgeois system. In 1789, the citadel of monarchism, France, fell to a similar Revolution, one that shook Europe to its foundations. Within a hundred years, virtually every monarchy in Europe had been destroyed. They were replaced with an economic and social system which allowed the new ruling class to consolidate its own position of privilege—the mode of production known as capitalism.

THREE: The Basis of Capitalism

The consolidation of each capitalist regime was accomplished through the phenomenon known as the Industrial Revolution. This economic changeover, which marks the transition from an agrarian feudal system to an industrial capitalist one, first took place in Britain, which was then the most economically advanced nation of its time. The Industrial Revolution quickly spread to engulf the entire capitalist world.

The introduction of machinery and the factory system during the Industrial Revolution brought about a profound change in capitalism.

Before, capitalist manufacture had been small-scale and limited. Most capitalists were merchants who imported commodities from elsewhere and sold them in Europe at a profit. Now, with the factory system, huge numbers of commodities could be manufactured for sale. As factories and industrial machinery grew in number, so too did the working laborers needed to run them. Thus, during this time, the rural peasantry and serfs began to fade from view, and the industrial working class assumed a central role in the capitalist system.

By 1840, the Industrial Revolution had swept across Europe. Capitalist systems were firmly established in Britain and France, and the rise of German nationalism under Bismarck would soon produce another capitalist state. The landed aristocracy and the serf laborers had largely vanished, and the capitalists and their working class adjuncts were the main features on the economic landscape. It was during this time that Karl Marx began his inquiry into the process of capitalist development.

Marx began his investigation as a student of the German philosopher Georg Hegel. While Hegel himself had died shortly before Marx began his philosophical inquiry, his ideas dominated German philosophy during the first half of the 19th century. Marx and a number of other students, known collectively as the "Young Hegelians", examined Marx's philosophy intently.

The most influential concept introduced by Hegel was that of the "dialectic". Dialectics as a philosophy holds that reality is a constantly flowing, interacting and changing continuum, in which everything that exists is in the process of both being what it is and of becoming something else.

This flowing process, Hegel asserted, was produced by the dialectical inter-relationship of entities. Most Marxists use the terms "thesis" and "anti-thesis" to describe this process. These two entities interpenetrate and modify each other, and in the end produce a completely different entity, termed the "synthesis". This synthesis then becomes the new thesis, to be in turn confronted by a new anti-thesis. The process thus continues.

Hegel coupled this dialectical process with the precepts of philosophical idealism to complete his theoretical outlook. As a philosophy, idealism holds that matter and the material world are illusory and transitory, merely imperfect reflections of underlying ideals.

By combining the precepts of dialectics with philosophical idealism, Hegel produced a theory of social development. According to Hegel, the ideas which guided reality were put into motion by the actions of humans, in the form of their social and political institutions. These ideas, however, were themselves in a constant state of flux as they merged dialectically. As the ideal bases changed, he concluded, so too did the social and political institutions which reflected them. Thus, Hegel saw reality as being the interaction of opposing ideas to produce new ideas, with these ideological changes then being reflected in the structure of the political state and social relationships. An old idea of "justice", for instance, merged with new ideas to form a new concept of "justice", and social reality in turn was changed to conform to this new understanding.

A number of Young Hegelians soon abandoned this outlook. A Young Hegelian named Ludwig Feuerbach soon emerged as one of the leading proponents of philosophical materialism. Materialism as a philosophy holds that ideas are an illusion, and that material things are their own source of reality. Reality, materialism asserts, is subject to strict and unchanging "natural laws", which govern all things according to a complex chain of cause and effect. Human actions or ideas are powerless to change these natural laws, and the human race is unable to influence the course of its destiny. All materialists assert, to a greater or lesser degree, that reality is determined by these laws of development, and that humans can do nothing more than slavishly follow a path that has already been charted for them.

After a period of study, Marx was led to reject the "mechanistic materialism" of Feuerbach. Such an outlook, he concluded, did not give sufficient weight to humanity's own ability to influence the course of its development through ideas, reason and action.

At the same time, Marx was forced to jettison the idealism of Hegel, saying that ideas meant nothing if they were divorced from the reality within which they operated. Hegel and the other idealists, he declared, had failed to recognize that all ideas and philosophies are merely abstractions from reality. To Marx, it seemed as though the idealists depended too much on what they thought reality was instead of what they could see reality to be.

To escape this dilemma, Marx adopted the philosophical outlook which would later come to be known as "naturalism" (although Marx always continued to refer to it as "materialism" to distinguish it from Hegel's thought). As a philosophical outlook, naturalism asserts that nothing exists which is outside of the natural system. Idea and matter were each essential to the functioning of the natural process, and neither one could exist independently of the other.

Human ideas and desires could influence the course of social reality, Marx concluded, but only to the extent that those ideas and desires were applicable to reality. In the Marxian conception, the actions and ideas of humanity influenced the development of reality to the same extent as the conditions of reality produced new actions and ideas. The two sides are dialectically interpenetrating.

Thus, Marx concluded, a serious study of human society must begin with the study of actual human conditions. Since the most basic function of any group of human beings is to stay alive and reproduce, Marx concluded that the largest factor influencing human actions were those steps taken to produce food, shelter and other necessities, how these necessities were distributed among the members of the group, and how this pattern of production was able to maintain itself. This is the major focus of the science of economics (or, as it was known in Marx's day, "political economy"). Thus, Marx concluded, the basic reasons for human actions are found in the economic and social system by which they reproduce their lives, or, in Marx's terminology, in their "mode of production".

Marx thus began a period of intensive study of political economy, and pored over the works of classical economists such as Smith, Ricardo, and Say. From this study, it became obvious to Marx that every mode of production which had appeared in human history had divided people into various sections, each composed of people who performed similar socio-economic functions. Feudal society was divided into serfs (who labored to produce the wealth of society) and the aristocracy (which lived by appropriating the output of the serfs). The capitalist mode of production, Marx realized, was being divided into two groups; the capitalists (who own the machinery of production) and the working class (which owns nothing more than its ability to perform labor). Marx called these distinct socio-economic groupings "classes".

Here, Marx concluded, was the Hegelian dialectic at work. Throughout human history, the existing mode of production was marked by the opposed interests of differing classes. The synthesis of this struggle led to a new and different mode of production, which in turn produced its own class struggles and its own dialectical development. In this manner, the class struggle between the feudal aristocrats and the industrial merchants led to the destruction of the feudal system and the rise of the capitalists. The new mode of production, however, was producing its own class struggle in the form of the capitalist owners and the working class. According to the dialectic, these classes would eventually produce a new mode of production, which would develop from the internal conflicts and contradictions of the present system.

This conception of social development would later become known as "dialectical materialism", although Marx himself never used this term and, as we have seen, Marx was a naturalist and not a materialist. For the first half of his life, Marx's writings concerned themselves with pointing out the inadequacies of the materialist and idealist outlooks and with promoting his own naturalist and dialectical outlook. It was not until he began research for his giant work *Capital* that Marx began to systematically apply his conceptions of class warfare and dialectical development to the capitalist system.

In the earlier modes of production, such as the tribalism practiced by ancient hunter/gatherer societies, the production of economic goods was motivated solely by the need for them. The hunter/gatherer made baskets, pottery, weapons and other implements simply because they were needed by individuals for their utility, or, as Marx put it, for their "use-value".

In hunter/gatherer economies, the exchange of products only occurs on occasions when the trading partners each have a temporary surplus of something and can afford to trade it away. As commodity production became more prevalent under feudalism, however, certain individuals began to specialize in specific items—weapons, pottery, cloth. These objects had only a limited use-value to their producer; their value lay chiefly in the ability of the producer to exchange them for other objects. The production of these "exchange-values" was in turn greatly aided by the introduction of money as a medium of exchange.

This marks the beginning of the commodity economic relationship. A commodity, in the Marxian sense, is simply any object which is produced for its exchange-value rather than its use-value. Under the simplest commodity exchange system, the economic relationship follows the formula:

$$C-M-C$$

where C represents a commodity and M is the monetary medium of exchange. In this relationship, the producer makes a particular commodity C and converts its exchange-value into the corresponding sum of money by selling it. This money, in turn, can at any time be converted by exchange into any desired commodity C.

As the capitalist system developed within the limits of feudalism, however, this formula began to be drastically altered. Those merchants in the feudal economy who were able to acquire large amounts of money (usually through the conquest and plunder of foreign colonies) found that they were able to use this ready cash to procure commodities which, instead of being sold for the purpose of later purchase of desired commodities, could be sold simply to produce more money for the production of new exchange-values, which in turn could be sold for more money. In this manner, the role of money is altered—it is no longer a simple means of exchange; it is transformed into a means of creating and expanding wealth. Money has become capital.

In the capitalist economic relationship. the formula is:

$$M—C—M'$$

where M is the original capital invested in production, C is the exchange-value which is produced, and M' (pronounced "M-prime") is the money resulting from the sale of this exchange-value.

If M' is the same as M, the capitalist gains nothing from the transaction; he merely regains his original outlay. Therefore, the aim of the capitalist is to increase the value of M' and to make the difference between M and M' as large as possible, thereby finishing the process with more money than he started with.

It is important to realize the difference between this economic relationship and the earlier simple commodity relationship. Even in the capitalist economy, laborers and other non-capitalists still follow the C—M—C formula; that is, they sell one commodity (their own labor power) to the capitalist in exchange for a sum of money M. This money is then exchanged for a desired use-value C. No new wealth is created in this relationship—it is merely changed in form.

The capitalist formula of M—C—M' is very different. The capitalist does not sell his commodities merely to obtain money to exchange for other commodities. Rather than simply selling in order to buy something else, the capitalist aims to create new wealth. He buys commodities in order to sell them for more money than he used to buy them.

The key to understanding the capitalist mode of production lies within this process of creating and expanding wealth. Since the M' realized at the end of the capitalist exchange relationship is larger than the M capital originally invested in production, we are forced to ask where the added value comes from—that is, how is the original sum M transformed into the higher sum M'? The answer to this lies in Marx's "labor" method of measuring value.

In any production process, the first step is to assemble in one place all of the materials needed for production. If one wishes to make a chair, for example, one must gather the leather, wood, upholstery, and any other materials which are to go into the chair. If this process is to be carried out with the aid of machinery, this equipment must also be procured and provided with the lubricants, electricity, fuel or anything else it needs to operate.

But, it is obvious, these gathered materials will never produce a new chair all by themselves. Left to sit in a corner, unacted upon, they will forever remain a scattered pile of wood and other materials. Only when the materials are acted upon by human labor can they be transformed into a chair. Thus, the element that makes the completed chair more useful than the materials that went into it is the addition of human labor power.

This holds true whether the commodity to be produced is a chair, a jet airliner or a piece of literature (since human brain-power must be expended to produce literature). All economic commodities can therefore be viewed as "solidified labor", and all commodities take their value from the labor which produces them.

Further, since all commodities can be compared according to the amount of labor time which is necessary to produce them, it is obvious that the value of commodities is directly related to the necessary amount of labor power they require to be produced. A product requiring six hours of work to produce, for instance, is twice as valuable (or, to put it another way, twice as costly to produce in terms of expended labor) as one containing only three hours, and three times as valuable as one requiring only two hours.

These commodities will therefore exchange in such a way that the exchanged labor values are equal. Suppose, for instance, that it normally takes a potter one hour to produce a bowl, while a carpenter, using socially available methods, takes three hours to make a chair. The carpenter would not agree to exchange his chair for just one bowl, since he would then be exchanging three hours of work for only one hour. It would be more advantageous for the carpenter to simply keep his chair and expend one hour of work to make his own bowl. Therefore, the carpenter will exchange his chair for three bowls, three hours of labor value for three hours of labor value. In this example, we could say that one chair is worth three bowls.

The use of machinery in the factory system makes it easier for human labor power to produce commodities, but it does nothing to alter the basic measurement of value. Using machinery and equipment, for example, the potter may be able to produce a bowl in just ten minutes instead of an hour. This machinery, however, is itself the product of human labor, and must first be produced before the potter can use it. Thus, the labor value of the bowl now contains not only the ten minutes of labor needed to actually manufacture it, but also a portion of the labor power necessary to produce the machinery used in the manufacturing process. If, in its lifetime, this machine produces a million bowls, each bowl contains one-millionth of the total labor power used to produce the machine. This gradual transfer of value from machinery to commodity is recognized in the capitalist concept of "depreciation".

Of course, the argument could be made that it is not proper to compare labor power in this manner, since some workers are more skilled, and therefore more valuable, than others. This argument does not, however, contradict the labor method of measuring value. Skilled labor is more valuable simply because more effort was expended in educating and training the skilled worker; i.e., the skilled laborer embodies a higher proportion of human brain power.

Moreover, in the capitalist factory system, the distinction between "skilled" and "unskilled" workers gradually loses its meaning, since the assembly line and mechanization tend to reduce all production tasks to the simple repetition of easily-learned movements. Workers on an automobile assembly line, for instance, do nothing more than bolt one piece onto the assembly as it moves down the line before them. Workers in an assembly plant are in essence interchangeable, and can be moved from task to task with little training.

This interchangeability of labor can also be seen in the rise of the "temporary employment service". For a fee, capitalists can hire workers for short-term assignments from a central "pool". These tasks are so simple that temporary workers are able to move from one enterprise to another with little or no training. This is true even of clerical or "white collar" workers, since the introduction of computerized equipment has reduced the tasks of most of these workers to simple keyboard entry.

Marx thus asserted that labor under capitalism is reduced to "abstract labor". It is a mere commodity, as necessary for running the capitalist's factories as are machinery, raw materials and utilities. Workers under capitalism are not people—they are merely another expense which the capitalist must pay if he is to continue to expand his capital and make money. Workers are no different from a computer terminal, a conveyor belt or a shovel—the capitalist buys laborers, uses them until they wear out or break down or become obsolete, then he throws them away and buys new ones.

It is within this commodity relationship, the capitalist's purchase of human labor power as a commodity, that we can determine the source of the extra value created by the capitalist production process—of the difference between M and M'.

The value of any commodity can be measured according to the amount of labor which is necessary to produce it. Human labor power comes from human beings, and in order to produce human beings we need food, shelter, clothing, etc. Thus, the amount of labor necessary to produce human labor as a commodity is equal to the amount of labor needed to produce all of the various things which the worker uses in his life.

Since the food, clothing, etc., used by the workers are themselves the products of human labor, it follows that some definite amount of labor time is required to produce all of these various things, and that this labor time represents the labor value of the worker's labor power. Let us say that the time necessary to produce all of these things is five hours; in other words, it takes five hours a day to produce "one day's worth" of the worker's living.

If the exchange relationship between the worker and the capitalist were equal, the laborer would exchange five hours of labor for five hours of labor value (in its monetary wage equivalent). However, the worker is compelled to work in the capitalist's factory not for merely five hours, but for eight. In this extra three hours, the worker continues to expend labor and produces new value above and beyond the five hours of value he receives in wages. In essence, he gives up eight hours of labor time, but receives only five hours in exchange for it. The surplus value which is created, the three "extra" hours of work, are appropriated by the capitalist.

Some readers may find this process easier to understand if we picture it in monetary terms rather than in labor value terms. Since labor power as a commodity can also be expressed in its monetary form, this does not change at all the essence of what we are saying.

Suppose that, in order to obtain the things which are socially accepted as being necessary to make a living, the worker must receive a wage of $5 an hour. The exchange-value of the commodity produced in the factory (as determined by the capitalist marketplace) is $20. Suppose it takes one hour for the worker to produce each commodity, and that each commodity requires $5 worth of raw materials and $3 in depreciated machinery. Thus, in one hour, the worker's labor power transforms $8 worth of raw materials and machinery into $20 worth of commodity. In other words, the worker's labor has created $12 worth of value.

For this $12 worth of created value, however, the worker is only paid $5 by the capitalist. The difference between the value created by the worker and the wage value he receives in exchange for it is $7, which goes directly into the capitalist's pocket. It is the surplus value, the difference between the M capital laid out by the business owner and the M' taken in by him. This difference is created solely by the capitalist not paying the worker for the full value of his work. In essence, the capitalist compels the laborer to work under the agreement, "I'll give you $5 if you give me $12."

Since the labor value necessary to produce the machinery and materials for production is fixed at the beginning of the production process, and transfers this value to the commodities at a constant rate, this value is referred to in Marxian economics as "constant capital". Wages and other employee compensations, which are subject to change from one production run to another, are referred to as "variable capital". Thus, the total value of a commodity in a capitalist system is:

$$\text{total value} = C + V + S$$

where C is the amount paid for the machinery and raw materials (constant capital), V represents wages and employee benefits (variable capital) and S equals the surplus value appropriated by the capitalist. This formula, it can be seen, is similar to the financial statements put out by capitalist businessmen, in which total value is listed as gross revenues, constant capital is listed as materials, physical plant and depreciation, variable capital is shown as wages and benefits, and surplus value is shown as gross profits.

To the charge that he makes his living by appropriating a portion of the value created by his workers, the capitalist is apt to respond, "But I deserve a share of the profits, because I am the one who is risking my capital, and I am the one who is providing the management know-how to run the business." In reality, this claim is nonsense. Since the capitalist produces no new wealth and creates no new value, all of the money which he invests has as its source some prior exploitation of labor (unless the capitalist has a printing press in his basement and prints his own money). As for the contention that the capitalist's profit is a reward for his managerial skills, modern corporate practice, as we shall soon see, has already eliminated this argument.

A portion of the surplus value which the capitalist appropriates is used to purchase the use-values which he needs or wants, but the major portion of this surplus value is reinvested into his capital. This reinvestment expands the sum M and in turn increases M', thus producing more surplus value for re-capitalization and re-investment. This process of accumulation, of continuously investing more money in order to make still more money, is the driving force of capitalism. Thus, whether he wants to or not, the capitalist is driven to continuously expand his capital in order to maintain his position as a capitalist.

There are three ways in which the capitalist can increase the amount of surplus value extracted from the workers: (1) he can lengthen the working day to produce more hours of unpaid surplus labor, (2) he can use machinery and improved production methods to increase the productivity of the work force, thus reducing the number of hours necessary to reproduce the workers' wages, or (3) he can take over and absorb the capital of some smaller enterprise, thereby expanding his capital supply.

In practice, the organized labor movement has tended to rule out the first option (although in pre-union days it was common for business owners to increase the length of the working day to twelve or fourteen hours). The second option (the "speed-up") allows the capitalist to produce more commodities cheaper, and thus to capture a larger share of the market. In addition, smaller capitalists cannot afford to invest as much in improved machinery and mechanization, and thus fall in competition with those who can. This makes the third option all the more easier.

The early stages of capitalism are thus characterized by ruthless cutthroat competition, as each individual capitalist tries at all costs to eliminate his competitors and seize their capital. In their quest to expand surplus value, the capitalists scramble over each other's corpses to get to the top.

In this process of ruthless competition, however, the groundwork is laid for a new stage of the capitalist system—the gradual elimination of competition.

FOUR: Monopoly Capitalism

At first, the battle between the capitalists begins on roughly equal terms. As certain capitalists begin to gain a slight advantage, however, the character of the race changes. If a certain business owner is able to introduce new machinery or technology, for example, he will be able to increase the productivity of his workers, and thus push the price level of his commodities lower and capture a larger share of the market.

Using the example given earlier, for instance, let us assume that the capitalist is able to introduce new machinery capable of producing two commodities per hour instead of just one. Now, he is able to use $10 in raw materials, $4 in depreciated machinery (we assume that the new machinery is more expensive than the old) and $5 in wages to produce two commodities with a combined value of $40. The surplus value is now $21 instead of the earlier $7.

This capitalist can thus afford to pay higher wages in order to avoid labor unrest. More importantly, he is able to lower his selling price per commodity while still maintaining a high profit rate, thus underselling his competitors and expanding his market.

Capitalists who cannot afford the higher outlay for constant capital will inevitably lose the race and drop out. The ever-increasing amount of capital needed to obtain state-of-the-art technology makes it more and more difficult for new competitors to arise in place of the old ones. Thus, the gradual result is the death by attrition of most competition, and the survival of an ever-decreasing number of larger and larger capitals.

This process can be seen in virtually every industry. In every economic sphere of capitalist society, the market is dominated by a tiny handful of huge capital conglomerates which easily crush all attempts at competition. The handful of automobile manufacturers (the Big Three) and the small number of oil companies (the Seven Sisters) which dominate their industries are but the most well-known examples.

Thus, capitalist competition inexorably produces a situation in which competition virtually disappears. While this state of affairs should properly be referred to as an "oligopoly" (where a handful of enterprises controls the industry), rather than a "monopoly" (where one enterprise dominates), the term "monopoly" has become so widely used that we will continue to use it here.

One of the most important tools in this centralization of capital is the joint stock company or corporation. Corporations are formed when a number of capitalists agree to unify their capital under a joint management. This has the effect of greatly increasing the capital resources available to the enterprise, enabling it to invest heavily and expand rapidly where smaller capitals cannot. For instance, ten capitalists with $1 million each in individual capital can unify these into a joint stock company with $10 million in capital. Since this larger capital is capable of much faster growth and greater accumulation than a series of individual capitals would be, it is more efficiently able to overcome competition and increase surplus value than its individual components could. These higher surpluses can then be divided up among the consortium of capitalists who make up the corporation, in the form of "dividends".

Since the joint stock may be owned, in small blocks, by literally thousands of people, it may appear as though the corporation decentralizes the ownership and control of capital. Many corporate officials have made this argument, asserting that we have entered an age of "people's capitalism", in which the control of wealth is being spread democratically to the masses of working people through stock ownership. In reality, this contention is nonsense. The corporate structure only serves to centralize greater control of capital in fewer and fewer hands.

According to the principles of corporate operation, the shareholder or consortium of shareholders who owns a controlling interest of the capital stock (legally, this is 51%, but in practice it can fall to as low as 25% or even 10%) is given decision-making power over all of the rest of the corporation's joint stock, no matter how many other individual stockholders there might be. Further, when we remember the fact that the major stockholder in a corporation may in fact be another corporation, we can see that the control of stock may stretch tentacle-like over huge distances.

For instance, let us suppose that Capitalist Jones owns 51% of the stock in Corporation A, and that A has a capital of $2 billion. Corporation B has capital of $3 billion, and is 51% owned by Corporation A. Corporation C has $2 billion in capital and is likewise 51% held by Corporation B.

The centralization is apparent. By virtue of his owning 51% of one company, our individual capitalist in effect has control over all three corporations and their combined capital of $7 billion. His controlling interest in the first company, which controls the second, which in turn controls the third, centralizes the control of all three companies and all of its individual stock shares into the hands of one man—Capitalist Jones.

Capitalist Jones is in an enviable position. By agreeing to return a portion of the surplus value in the form of dividends, he gains access to capitals which are far beyond his individual means, allowing him to enrich himself even more efficiently. And, since the ownership of corporate stock is itself virtually monopolized by a handful of wealthy capitalists (historically in the US, the top 2% of the population has always owned 50-60% of all corporate stock), Capitalist Jones has very few competitors who can wrest control of these assets from him.

Thus, rather than "democratizing" the economy, the joint stock company only centralizes it further. As a side effect, the joint stock company, with its agreed-upon joint management, has in effect removed the controlling capitalists from the sphere of production. The actual day-to-day management of the corporation is left to a team of hired executives, managers and directors, who are responsible solely to "the stockholders" —i.e., to Capitalist Jones.

This managerial apparatus is not in itself capitalist— that is, it does not extract any surplus value by virtue of owning capital. It is true that, in many corporations, the major shareholders are themselves members of the managerial apparatus, but this is peripheral to their role as capitalists. To the extent that the managers or executive officers of a corporation are not in themselves the major shareholder, they cannot be viewed as capitalists in the strict sense of the term (although they are certainly capitalist in their outlooks and value systems). They are merely "hired guns" who manage the capitalist's interests for him in exchange for part of the spoils.

The popular distinction between "labor" and "capital" as being "those who work" as opposed to "those who don't" here reaches its clearest form. The corporate capitalist, besides performing no labor in the process of production, now is not required to take part in directing or managing it either. As he does with the laborer, he merely buys the ability of somebody else to do this for him. In essence, the corporate capitalist simply sits back and lets other people produce his living for him. His living comes, not from his "management skills", nor from his "entrepreneurship", nor from his "superior business acumen" —it comes solely from the fact that he, and he alone, owns capital.

The huge masses of capital created by the joint stock company quickly propel it to the pinnacle of economic power. If the normal competitive process were allowed to play itself out, there would eventually be one corporation controlling each industry, until finally all of society's productive forces would be taken over and monopolized by a single octopus-like corporate conglomerate.

In reality, the process is halted long before this point is reached, by the capitalists themselves. Once a handful of large corporations grow to dominate the industry, the competitive process becomes too destructive to each company. Since the corporation's constant capital costs and its outlays for management and distribution soon grow to huge levels, competition which leads to lower prices may push profits below the levels needed to pay for these relatively fixed costs.

To avoid this danger, the monopolist corporations agree between themselves to swear off direct price competition and to instead divide the market amongst themselves in the form of a trust or cartel, which provides a *modus vivendi* for the capitalists. Now, instead of "live and let die" competition, the cartel allows the monopolists to settle their scores in a "live and let live" arrangement.

This does not mean, by any stretch of the imagination, that the individual members of the cartel are any less hostile to one another. Indeed, in the event that a crisis or unexpected setback cripples one member of the cartel, the others would lose no time in falling on it like a pack of piranha, dismembering and consuming their erstwhile partner. For the most part, this does not happen because no member of the cartel is strong enough to deal a fatal blow to its counterpart without risking a lethal retaliation.

Under monopoly capitalism, partial control over the supply of commodities allows the capitalists to charge prices which are higher than the value of the commodities, thus increasing their rate of profit. Earlier, we assumed that the commodities which were produced by capitalists were exchanged at their labor value, and that the final monetary equivalent of this value was determined in the capitalist marketplace. To understand the monopoly pricing system, we must examine this capitalist market relationship in more detail.

When the available supply of a commodity is larger than the demand for its exchange-value, we could say that its labor value is "too high", i.e., too much labor power was expended to produce these commodities. Since effective demand is unable or unwilling to absorb this supply, a portion of this total value must be considered as "socially unnecessary". In turn, the exchange value of these commodities ("price") will be realized, not at the higher level of labor power which they actually contain, but only at that fraction which is socially necessary. In other words, the actual price received in the exchange of these commodities will be less than it would have been if all of the commodities had been socially necessary.

When the supply of commodities is lower than the demand for them, however, the situation is reversed. Now, "too little" labor power has been expended, and the value of exchange is temporarily higher than the labor value actually embodied in these commodities. Surplus value on these commodities is higher than normal.

Under conditions of competition, no individual enterprise is able to exert enough pressure on either the supply or the demand of a commodity to influence its price, and commodity prices tend to fluctuate around their actual labor value. Under monopoly conditions, however, such an influence is possible.

Within a competitive capitalist system, profit rates tend to be the same everywhere, since, if extra high profits were to be made in a particular industry or sphere of the economy, small mobile capitals will flow into that area, increasing the labor value invested in the total output and pushing it closer to the level which is socially necessary. In other words, high-profit industries will attract other capitalists, increasing the supply and lowering prices until the average rate of profit has once again been established.

Thus, the selling price of any commodity can be viewed as the cost of production (constant capital plus variable capital) plus a surplus which is equal to the average rate of profit. If the average rate of profit is, say, 20%, the capitalist will set a price such that his investment will return an average of 20%.

Overproduction or underproduction of the commodity, then, has the effect of raising or lowering the additional amount over the cost of production which is actually realized as surplus value. The marketplace can therefore be viewed as the capitalist mechanism for determining how much expended labor power is actually "socially necessary".

Capitalists who set their prices high so as to realize a higher profit rate—say, 45% instead of 20%—will only be able to realize this extra profit if all other producers do the same. Otherwise, other producers will sell their commodities closer to their costs of production, thus underselling the higher-profit commodity and driving it from the market. Or, if capital is free to flow into this super-profitable industry, this new investment will lower prices until the average rate of profit is again established.

Monopolists, however, are able to distort this process and produce super-profits for themselves. The steadily-increasing costs of the machinery and technology needed to enter the monopolist industries tends to restrict the entry of outside capital. At the same time, the monopolist cartel has agreed among themselves to avoid competition through the method of underselling each other in price wars. Thus, the monopolists are free, within certain limits, to set their prices as much above their cost of production as they wish.

Of course, there are upper limits to the prices the oligarchists can charge. Although competition within the industry has come to a virtual end, the monopolists must be aware of competition between industries. If monopolists drive the price of steel higher than the purchasers can or will pay, these purchasers will abandon steel for cheaper aluminum or plastics. Also, if monopoly prices are set too high, monopolists from other nations who are not yet members of the cartel may move in and undersell in order to capture the market. Japanese monopolists in the auto and electronics industries have proven that they are even willing to sell at a loss for a time in order to penetrate and capture the American market, thus breaking the rules of the cartel and provoking monopolist cries of "unfair competition".

Within the monopoly cartel itself, moreover, the opportunity exists for certain members to obtain profit rates even higher than the average cartel super-profit. Suppose that three automobile manufacturers form a cartel, and their individual capitals are broken down as:

Company A:

4 million C + 1 million V + 1 million S = 6 million

Company B:

6 million C + 1.5 million V + 1.5 million S = 9 million

Company C:

8 million C + 2 million V + 2 million S = 12 million

Let us further assume that the total value of A is contained in 3000 automobiles (with a value of 2000 each), that B produces 4000 autos at 2250 each, and C produces 7000 with value of 1715 each.

In each enterprise, the profit rate is S/C + V, or 20%. The final selling price is determined by adding the cost of production (C+V) and the normal 20% profit. Thus, Company A will sell its cars at 2000, B at 2250 and C at 1715.

Under competitive conditions, it is obvious, Company C will be able to undersell the others and ruin the cartel. The only way to avoid this is to have all the members of the cartel sell their commodities at approximately the same price. (Since "price-fixing" is supposed to be illegal, most cartels instead use the "price leader" system, in which one member of the cartel— usually the strongest—announces a price increase, to be shortly after followed by similar increases by the other members of the cartel. In this manner, the fiction of "independent pricing through the marketplace" is maintained and pesky anti-trust actions are avoided.)

The cartel's agreed-upon price, however, must allow the least profitable member of the cartel to realize at least the average rate of profit. The weakest member in our example is Company B, which must sell its cars at a price of 2250 to realize a 20% profit. The cartel will, therefore, set its price at 2250 per unit.

Company B thus sells its 4000 cars at 2250 each and receives 9 million total, a surplus of 1.5 million. Company A, however, also sells its cars at 2250 each, and realizes a surplus of 1.75 million. Company C sells its cars at the same 2250 each, and realizes a surplus of 5.75 million. Company A's profit rate remains 20%, but B's has increased to 35% and C's has leaped to 57%.

In advanced monopoly economies, it proves to be a disadvantage for the cartel to continually re-invest its huge surplus values into expanded production in its own field of industry, since, as we shall see later, this aggravates the danger of overproduction and causes a fall in profits. Instead, the huge monopolies are forced to diversify their capital and invest in areas which are not at all related to their original industry. Thus we are led into the spectacle of tobacco companies owning food distributors, electric companies owning TV networks, and discount stores owning book chains.

This same quest for profits drives the monopolists to extend their reach overseas. The "undeveloped nations", with their cheap labor and untapped sources of cheap raw materials, produce a much higher rate of profit than does capital invested in the home country. The monopoly capitalist thus seeks to dominate this source of super-profits by establishing his own capital in these nations, where the superior productivity of his technology will dominate the market, crowding out and exterminating the indigenous capitalist enterprises. The monopolists soon establish de facto control over the foreign nation's economy, and proceed to suck it dry of raw materials and labor resources while repatriating the profits back to the home country.

Through trade with the undeveloped nations, the monopolists are able to realize huge surplus values. The enormous profitability of this trade lies in the fact that commodities are exchanged at the labor value represented by the time necessary to produce them—as measured from the point of view of the purchaser. In the undeveloped nation, with its lack of industrialization and mechanization, the amount of labor necessary to produce a single commodity will differ markedly from that in the industrialized nations.

In a non-industrialized nation, for instance, it may take a native three hours to produce 100 pounds of spun cotton. In industrialized nations using power machinery, it may take only one hour to produce the same 100 pounds. When natives sell their cotton to the industrial nation, therefore, they will receive, not the three hours of labor value which they put into it, but only the one hour of labor which is socially necessary for its production in the industrialized country.

Conversely, the finished clothing produced by the monopolist's machinery may take one hour of necessary labor, while the native with his hand loom may expend six hours to make the same piece of clothing. The industrialist is thus able to exchange the clothing to the native, not at the one hour of labor which was expended, but at the six hours of value which are socially necessary from the native's point of view.

The economic relationship between the monopolist and the native is inherently lopsided and exploitative. The native is forced by economic necessity to give up commodities for less value than was invested in them, and obtains the monopolist's commodities for a higher value than they contain.

In monetary terms, the picture looks like this: The native produces 100 pounds of cotton at a price of $15. The industrialist, however, can produce the same amount at a cost of just $5. Thus, if the native is to sell cotton in the industrialist's market, it must be sold at a competitive price— at a price of $5 rather than the $15 it is worth.

Similarly, if we assume that the monopolist can produce an item of clothing at a cost of $5 but the native must use a value of $30 to produce the same item, the industrialist can push his prices up to $30 and still be competitive with the native manufacturer. The native pays $30 for a piece of clothing rather than the $5 the monopolist would get for it in the industrialized country.

The native is thus cheated in the buying and in the selling, producing a steady supply of super-profits for the monopolist. The undeveloped nation is systematically drained of its wealth, and these profits flow back into the monopolist coffers.

This system forms the basis for "economic imperialism", in which capital is exported by the monopolist and super-profits are imported by him.

Naturally, the indigenous merchant class which is thus being crowded out of its own market will resist this intrusion, and the native government will attempt to shut the foreigners out with restrictive trade barriers, tariffs and quotas. It is in the interests of the monopolists to prevent this by installing a government which is friendly to the monopolists (or which can at any rate be influenced and manipulated by them).

Thus, the undeveloped country becomes an economic "neo-colony", ruled by a government which safeguards the interests of the foreign monopolists. In ancient China, this economic role was carried out by a class of bureaucrats known as compradors, and the puppet states set up by monopoly imperialists are known today as "comprador states".

To protect this comprador state against rival monopolists from other nations and from rival factions within the dominated neo-colony, the monopolists need the ability to use international diplomatic power to insure the political viability of the client state, and also the ability to use military force to defend the comprador state against internal and external opponents. The monopoly capitalists, on their own, are unable to provide these guarantees. But they do have a partner which can serve in this role, and which can further safeguard the status of the domestic monopoly cartel. This partner is the national government of the cartel's home nation.

Legally, the state is obligated by antitrust laws to prevent price-fixing and to break up cartels if they form. In reality, however, the complete domination of the state by monopoly capitalists insures that the interests of the monopolists are protected by the government. The widespread presence of corporate officers in high government positions and the almost total domination of the election process by moneyed interests demonstrates the Siamese-twin-like relationship between the national government and the national economic elite.

The national state, then, is in reality a junior partner of the monopoly interests, and it protects and supports the profits and privileges of the corporate capitalists. It is no accident that, as it was originally written, the US Constitution granted the right to vote only to white male property-owners. It was only after the moneyed interests had gained domination over the electoral process (and after they had been pressured into it by organized resistance) that non-property owners were granted the privilege of voting. Since the monopolists dominate the electoral process, this privilege in essence decides nothing more than which of two white middle-aged wealthy property-owners would get to administrate the corporate system for the next four years.

Throughout history, the power of the state has consistently shown itself to be at the disposal of the monopolists. During the bitter wars against unionization in the late 19th and early 20th centuries, the military force of the state was again and again called upon to break strikes, suppress local organizing attempts and attack unionists, thus propping up the interests of the capitalists against those of the workers.

Even those areas of state intervention in the economy which are widely viewed as being in the interests of the workers often had the real goal of propping up the monopolists. Programs such as unemployment insurance, worker's compensation, the abolition of child labor, or the eight-hour work day were not granted out of the goodness of the corporate heart. These programs (all of which were labeled as "socialistic" by the monopolists) were forced upon a resisting business elite by bloody strikes and insurrections led by organized labor. It did not take long for the monopolists to realize that, if they did not give in and make some concessions, the workers would pick up guns and take *everything*. So the capitalists gave up a little in order to save the rest. If things are to remain the same, the saying goes, they will have to change.

In other instances, the state props up capitalist interests by direct control of selected corporate enterprises. In the popular view, "socialism" simply means the government ownership of industry. It can be seen, however, that government ownership of industry in the monopolist nations is not at all "socialistic", but is solely intended to prop up the existing order.

The industries which are most often placed under government ownership are the transportation and utilities networks. These industries are vital to all capitalists, since they determine the way in which commodities are produced and taken to market. If these vital industries were in the hands of private owners, it would represent a mortal threat to all other capitalists. If the electric industry were in the hands of a private monopolist, for instance, the capitalist who controlled it would be able to cut off the supply of power to any capitalist at will. Similarly, private owners of transportation networks can restrict the access of any capitalist to market. Thus, the monopolists who controlled these key industries would have virtual power of blackmail over the entire capitalist structure—by driving up the prices for their services, they could ruin anyone they desired.

The solution to this threat has been to place such key industries under the control of the state, which is free from the interests of any single capitalist but not free from the interests of the capitalist system as a whole.

In many instances, the state will also intervene in a declining industry which is important to the national economy as a whole. Huge corporations may extend their tentacles into virtually the whole economic system, and a crisis in such a corporation inevitably has a ripple effect which will impact the whole economy. The automobile industry, for instance, has been calculated to consume as much as one-third of the US economy. If a major auto manufacturer falters, the resulting crisis will grow to encompass the other industries which are largely dependent upon the auto industry, such as steel, rubber, glass and electronics. These in turn produce declines in secondary industries such as ore mining, oil drilling, etc. Thus, the fallout from a single economic failure may impact virtually the whole national economy, dragging everybody else down along with the unfortunate corporate failure.

This threat to everyone's profits is, once again, dealt with through the intervention of the state. To prevent the failure of an important corporate conglomerate, the government will use loans or subsidies to guarantee that the industry remains profitable. In extreme cases, the state itself will be forced to take over the administration of the enterprise in order to insure its continued survival. Examples of these kinds of state intervention are the US government bailouts of Lockheed and Chrysler and the nationalization of key industries by the British and French governments.

The most important role which the state plays in monopoly capitalism, however, is in foreign economic expansion through neo-colonies. The government actively uses its political and military strength to protect the foreign interests of the monopoly corporations. Government diplomatic ties establish and legitimize the comprador states demanded by the needs of international capital. State economic aid to the comprador nation ties it directly into the monopolist financial system. State military power defends the comprador government from internal subversion and from the predations of rival imperialist blocs.

Thus, the highest stage of capitalist development is that of economic imperialism. In this stage, capital is fully centralized into monopolistic corporations which do away with the competition associated with earlier capitalism. The need for these monopolists to expand their interests overseas brings the already close ties between the economic elite and the political elite even closer, as the power of the national government is used to insure the economic and political domination of the neo-colony.

It is this mad scramble to expand profits, however, that sets the stage for increasingly sharper contradictions and crises which cripple the monopolist system. Eventually, these stresses will become too great, and the monopolist system will meet its doom.

FIVE: Contradictions and Crises

The most obvious of the stresses and internal conflicts in the monopolist system can be seen in the global scramble for neo-colonies and in the militarization needed to support this scramble. The monopolist who attempts to dominate a foreign comprador regime will be met and opposed by rival international capitalists, who are driven by the same imperatives to expand their own sources of profit. This economic struggle for control of markets is invariably reflected in the military sphere as well, as the respective national states come to the aid of their own monopoly capitalists. Thus, conflicts, wars and tensions will arise over which monopoly nation will dominate this or that neo-colony. The Spanish-American War, both World Wars, and nearly every war since, were all fought over the question of who would control the world's economic neo-colonies.

After the monopolists have divided up all of the world's neo-colonies into stable shares ("spheres of influence"), the only possible readjustments take the form of the seizure of one imperialist's neo-colonies by another. In extreme cases, this may take the form of direct military conquest, as it did when the US seized Cuba and the Philippines from Spain, Germany seized Alsace-Lorraine from France and Japan seized the British and Dutch colonies in Southeast Asia. Conflict and war are inevitable as stronger monopolists attempt to wrest control of desirable areas from weaker imperialists.

Thus, the non-industrialized "Third World" serves unwillingly as the battleground for rival imperialist blocs, who are driven by economic necessity to wage war in order to expand their sources of profit. World peace is impossible under monopoly capitalism—not because the leaders of these nations are aggressive or evil, but because they are the victims of an economic system which must be expansionistic in order to survive.

At the same time, the capitalist system is steadily weakened by stresses and strains which arise within its own structures. We will study these stresses in some detail, since, although their basic roots remain the same, these crises are manifested differently at varying levels of capitalist development.

In early competitive capitalism, crises manifest themselves most often in the form of "disproportionality". This is a function of the planless, haphazard process of capitalist production. The price of a commodity is determined by the interaction of supply and demand, but, in the capitalist system, each individual producer operates with insufficient knowledge concerning either of these two factors.

In the absence of a planned economy, the capitalist is forced to estimate as best he can the demand for his commodity. This estimate, however, is seldom accurate. And, because each manufacturer produces as an isolated entity, the capitalist has no way of knowing what the total supply of a commodity will be, since he cannot know the amounts of commodities which will be produced by other manufacturers. The result is a constant fluctuation of prices, since the capitalists consistently produce "too much" or "too little" supply for the current demand.

These fluctuations in exchange-value are dangerous to the capitalist, since changes in price directly affect the proportion of surplus value which the capitalist is able to realize. If prices fall too low, the capitalist will be unable to realize any surplus value at all, and will lose a portion of his capital.

The disproportionality crisis results from this inability of the capitalist to rationally match the needed supply with the given demand. Because of this "anarchy of production", it is a mere happy coincidence when supply does match demand. The normal situation is for prices to fluctuate around the value of the commodity.

Once the stage of monopoly capitalism has been reached and industries are dominated by large oligarchies, however, the character of these crises changes. This new form of crisis is known as "overproduction".

The machinery and technological progress introduced by capitalism are, it is obvious, greater than those of any other economic system hitherto in existence. The productive abilities of modern monopoly capitalism are astounding, and are capable of turning out commodities at a rate which would astonish our feudal predecessors. As the productivity of human labor continues to be increased by monopolist technology, the capabilities of these productive forces will continue to expand enormously.

Once the production of commodities reaches a certain level, however, it outruns the ability of the market to absorb these commodities. In order for the monopolist to realize all of his surplus value, he must be able to sell all of the commodities which contain it. The monopolist who is able to produce a million toasters, for instance, cannot realize any profit at all unless he is able to sell them.

In classical capitalist economics, total income is assumed to always equal total costs, since every "cost" paid out by the capitalist is somebody else's "income". The money paid for raw materials or production equipment, for example, is in turn used as wages for the workers who produce them, allowing these workers to purchase other commodities which the economy produces. In theory, then, effective demand in a capitalist economy is always capable of absorbing the effective supply.

The super-profits of the monopoly system, however, combined with the enormously high productivity of monopolist technology, upset this relationship. When the monopolist receives a higher income from profits and increased surplus value, his effective demand for commodities does not increase at the same rate. This is a function of one of the primary characteristics of the capitalist system—the capitalist does not produce commodities for use-value, he produces only for exchange-value. In other words, the capitalist does not sell products in order to obtain money to buy the things he wants – instead, he sells simply in order to have more money to produce more commodities for sale. Of his profits, only a small portion are used to buy commodities which he wants for their use-value. The majority of the surplus value is instead reinvested back into more productive capability, which in turn produces still higher profits for him.

As more surplus is appropriated by the monopolist, and as the productivity of the economy continues to rise, an inherent contradiction begins to make itself felt. Increased investment in productive ability leads to an increased number of commodities. These commodities are not given away for free, however; they are only exchanged if they can be sold. The capitalist does not produce bread so that starving people can feed themselves; he produces bread to sell for a profit. If people have no money, they get no bread. The capitalist, after all, isn't in business to feed hungry people – he's in business to make money.

Since the income of non-capitalists is limited, and since in any case an increasing portion of the wealth goes to the monopoly capitalists, the ability of consumers to buy all of these commodities soon becomes severely limited, and productive capacity soon outpaces the effective demand. This "demand crunch" produces a glut in the market. It is important to keep in mind that this glut does not result from every consumer obtaining as many of these commodities as they need; it is caused by the unwillingness of the capitalist to exchange the commodity with anybody who does not have the money to pay for it.

The monopolist is thus left in a position in which he cannot sell all of the commodities which he is capable of producing. Faced with such a glut, it does no good for him to continue to reinvest his profits into expanded productive capacity, since he already cannot utilize the productive ability he has. Instead, under these circumstances, the monopolist simply chooses to save his capital until it can be reinvested profitably. In other words, this money is taken out of the process of capital circulation.

The effect of this is drastic. As this money is withdrawn from circulation, the purchasing power of workers in the production industries (who use these "costs" as wages) falls, aggravating the demand crunch and leading to further overproduction. This whole situation is caused by the growth of the monopolist's surplus value at a rate higher than he can find profitable ways to reinvest it. The monopolist quite literally has more money than he knows what to do with. As a result, he simply doesn't do *anything* with it.

The only way to restore this situation to profitability is to reduce productive capacity. In this way, the disproportion between supply and demand causes idled productive capacity, layoffs of workers, shutdowns of plants, and increased unemployment—in other words, a recession. The Great Depression resulted, in large part, because of the almost simultaneous appearance of this overproduction problem throughout the capitalist world. The same is true of the economic recession of the early 1990's. We can see that a progressively lower utilization of productive capacity (and with it a corresponding increase in the unemployment level) is an inherent feature of late monopoly capitalism.

This tendency towards overproduction can perhaps best be illustrated mathematically. The capitalist economy can be divided into two types of industries, those that manufacture consumer-oriented commodities (televisions, automobiles, food, etc.) and those that manufacture production-oriented commodities (factory machinery, computer systems, conveyor belts, etc.). Let us assume that the sector which produces productive machinery is called P, and the sector which produces consumer goods is called K. Then, the total value of the sector P is:

$$P = Cp + Vp + Sp$$

where P is the total value of the production sector, Cp is the total constant capital invested in this sector, Vp is the total variable capital, and Sp is the total surplus value produced. The total value of K, in turn, is:

$$K = Ck + Vk + Sk$$

where Ck, Vk and Sk are, respectively, the constant capital, variable capital and surplus value invested in consumer commodities.

The interaction of these two sectors is important to the capitalist system. To illustrate this relationship, let us first consider the case of simple reproduction, in which the expansion of productive capacity is not a goal; we assume that all values are merely to be reproduced, not increased. Under these conditions, we can safely assume that all surplus value is used by the capitalist to buy consumer goods.

The value to be created in the productive sector P must equal the total constant capital invested into both spheres of the economy, since all of the machinery and technology utilized in both sectors is produced by the P sector. Or, to put it another way, the total value of P must be enough to replace the depreciation of the total means of production used in the economy:

$$P = Cp + Ck$$

The total value produced by the consumer sector K, on the other hand, must be matched by the consumptive ability of the economy, in the form of wages and profits. Thus, the value of K must be equal to the total surplus values and variable capital of both sectors:

$$K = (Vk + Vp) + (Sk + Sp)$$

where K is the total consumer output, Vk + Vp is the total wage income for both sectors and Sk + Sp is the total profit income from both sectors.

So far, we have assumed that no expansion is made in the total values of P or K. In reality, however, the capitalist system is driven by a constant need to expand production. This expansion comes from reinvesting a portion of surplus value back into expanded productive ability. Thus, to fully understand this process, we must break down the total surplus value according to its use by the capitalist. Therefore:

$$Sk = Sk1 + Sk2 + Sk3$$

where Sk1 represents that portion of surplus value from the consumer sector which is used for the capitalist's own consumptive needs, Sk2 is that portion of surplus value which is earmarked for the purchase of additional constant capital, and Sk3 is that portion used for increasing variable capital. In other words, Sk1 goes for the capitalist's personal use, Sk2 is used to buy more machinery, and Sk3 is used to pay more workers. These same divisions are made in the P sector.

In simple reproduction, as we have seen, the productive capacity of P must exactly match the values of constant capital in both sectors. If the economy is to expand, however, the output of the productive sector P must be greater than the depreciation which results in both sectors, or:

$$P > Cp + Ck$$

In reality, P will increase according to the amount of new value that is invested in constant capital in both sectors:

$$P = Cp + Ck + Sp2 + Sk2$$

This gives the mathematical relationship:

$$Vp + Cp + Sp = Cp + Ck + Sp2 + Sk2$$

which can also be written as:

$$Vp + (Sp1 + Sp3) = Ck + Sk2$$

The left side of this equation is $Vp + (Sp1 + Sp3)$, where Vp is the production sector's total variable capital, $Sp3$ is that portion of surplus value which is reinvested into the production sector's variable capital, and $Sp1$ is that portion of the production sector's surplus value which is used for the capitalist's personal needs. In other words, it represents the total consumptive ability (demand) of the production sector of the economy.

The right side of this equation, on the other hand, is Ck + Sk2, where Ck is the total constant capital of the consumer section and Sk2 is additional constant capital investment from the consumer sector's surplus value. In other words, it represents the total productive ability (supply) of the consumer sector.

In its simplest form, then, this relationship indicates that, in order for production between the two sectors of the economy to be in equilibrium, the demand created by the production sector must be capable of absorbing the supply created by the consumer sector.

Since the tendency, under monopoly capitalism, towards the higher use of machinery and technology requires that a greater portion of capital is invested in constant capital rather than variable (in machinery rather than wages), and since the surplus value used for the capitalist's own consumption increases much more slowly than the total surplus value, the tendency is for the value of Sk2 in this equation to increase faster than either Sp1 or Sp3. This tends to produce the unequal relationship:

$$Vp + (Sp1 + Sp3) < Ck + Sk2$$

In other words, the productive ability of the consumer sector tends to grow faster than the consumptive ability of the production sector. This, in turn, upsets the equilibrium between these two sectors, and leads inexorably to the overproduction of commodities.

Given the anarchy of capitalist production, the monopolists have no way of rationally matching supply with demand, and no way of maintaining this equilibrium relationship. Further, since the operations of circulating capital from M to C and from C to M' (that is, the operations of buying and selling) are completely separated under capitalism, the monopolist has no way of knowing when this equilibrium has been disturbed until it is too late. By this time, the damage is already done—the market is glutted and invested capital can find no profitable outlet.

In fact, the widespread use of credit in the monopolist economy has made it more likely that the capitalist will continue to overproduce for a time. Since the capitalist can borrow the capital he needs for new investments, it is not necessary for him to realize the surplus value or profits from one production cycle before beginning another. Thus, he is able to continue his production despite the fact that he has not yet realized the surplus value from his previous production. This only deepens the overproduction crisis.

The monopolists are faced with a grave situation. Since it is impossible for the capitalist to sell all of his commodities, he must face the fact that a portion of his surplus value will be unrealizable—that is, it cannot be transformed from C to M'. Since capital is now no longer returning the average rate of profit, the monopolist has no choice but to cut back on his capital reinvestment. By bringing to a stop new investment in productive capacity and by idling those resources already present, the capitalist lowers the values of Ck and $Sk2$. The supply side of the equilibrium relationship now drops in relationship to the demand side, and a temporary balance is restored.

New increases in productivity, however, soon cause consumer output to rise again and eventually leads to another overproduction crisis. Once again, the capitalists are forced to idle productive capacity in order to continue to bring in the average rate of profit. Thus, the long-term tendency of monopoly capitalism is to periodically restrict the productive ability of the economy, and to progressively lower the rates of utilization of productive ability. Rather than producing a steady increase in productive ability, late monopoly capitalism is forced to produce a steady decline.

In order to extract himself from this lethal situation, the capitalist must find ways to increase his market and thus to dispose of those commodities which his productive ability can produce but which his market cannot absorb.

This can be done in several ways. One of the most common is that of "planned obsolescence", in which commodities are produced which are deliberately designed to wear out or break down quickly so they must be replaced. A commodity that is planned to last only half as long as its predecessor generates twice the effective demand, and twice the sales. This tactic has led to the widespread "throwaway society", in which everything from diapers to flashlights are disposable, producing a constant demand for replacements.

Another effective manner of expanding demand is through advertising. The entire huge networks of advertising and sales which are set up by the corporations are essentially nothing more than blatant attempts to create demand. By creating new commodities and then, through advertising ploys, convincing consumers that they need these commodities, effective demand is expanded.

As an added bonus, from the point of view of the monopolist, the advertising and sales networks create what could be called "nonproductive consumption", in which demand for commodities can be increased without a corresponding increase in supply. Advertising and sales people, for instance, do not produce any new commodities, but their salaries and wages can be used to purchase commodities, and thus help alleviate the problem of overproduction.

The largest player in this scheme is the so-called "welfare state". State programs such as welfare, food stamps and other transfer payments increase the purchasing power of consumers without adding to productive capacity, and thus help to counter the tendency towards overproduction. Non-consumer manufacturing, particularly the huge bloated military procurement network, also pay out huge salaries and wages, but the commodities produced by these networks are not consumer or production commodities, and thus do not aggravate the overproduction cycle.

Another factor that is of growing importance is the expansion of overseas markets. Until the onset of the monopolist overproduction crisis in the 1930's, the investment of capital overseas was concentrated in high-yield plantation agricultural products and in extractive industries such as oil or ores. Neo-colonies served largely as sources of cheap raw materials, and hardly at all as outlets for the capitalist's finished commodities.

Modern monopolists, however, faced with a recurring demand crunch, have been forced to turn their neo-colonial emphasis from cheap labor and resources into expanding markets for commodities. The monopolist who wishes to sell his commodities to the underdeveloped neo-colonies, however, quickly runs into an awkward problem—these neo-colonists have no money to spend on the monopolist's consumer commodities.

Thus, the imperialist monopolists now have no choice but to help these neo-colonies expand their income, thus enabling them to purchase the consumer commodities produced in the monopolist factories. Since the end of the Second World War, the international monetary system has embarked on a program of technical aid and financial backing to establish sources of income in the neo-colonies.

For the most part, this effort has been concentrated in such non-productive enterprises as communications, utilities and transportation. Productive enterprises have for the most part remained in monopolist hands, and thus pose no potential source of competition to the monopolist cartel. (Lately, the monopolists have begun moving productive factories to the neo-colonies on a large scale, but these factories are at all times owned and controlled by the monopolists). These enterprises expand the purchasing ability of the neo-colony (and also allow the monopolists to lower their variable capital investments), and thus help to offset the demand crunch.

Despite these palliatives, the overproduction crisis is never far away. In the 1970's, when military spending failed to play a large role, the tendency towards stagnation reappeared, as it did again in the early 1990's. Even in the "boom times", such as the early 1980's, full productive capacity is never utilized, and a growing portion of productive forces are idled and un-used (as reflected in the rising rate of acceptable "frictional" unemployment).

In the 1980's, the US tried to combat the overproduction crisis with a massive campaign of Keynesian debt spending, and succeeded in delaying the demand crunch. Unfortunately for the US monopolists, however, the huge budget deficit produced by this strategy resulted in a currency imbalance which made it easier for Japanese and European monopolists to enter the US market, undersell the US cartels, and snap up most of the demand thus created.

Thus, the continual increases in productive ability which are demanded by the needs of capital expansion routinely fall victim to the inability of the capitalist system to support this increased productive ability. Even during those times when productive ability is steadily increasing, another trend within the capitalist system eats away at this growth and eventually reverses it, returning the economy to its normal state of stagnation. This internal contradiction within capitalism centers around the rate of profit.

In his work *Capital*, Marx dwells at length on the problems posed to competitive capitalism by the rate of profit. As the capitalist system develops, the crises associated with the rate of profit tend to change in character. It is therefore worthwhile taking a look at how Marx assessed the problem of profit rates in competitive capitalism.

A few definitions are necessary first. The rate of profit is defined as the proportion of surplus value to the amount of capital needed to produce it, or:

$$P = S \,/\, C + V$$

The rate of surplus value is the proportion of surplus value generated to the amount of variable capital used to produce it, or:

$$S' = S / V$$

The degree of industrialization of the economy is known in Marxian terms as the "organic composition of capital", and is commonly represented by the letter Q. Q consists of the proportion of constant capital to total capital, or:

$$Q = C / C + V$$

From these definitions, we can derive the mathematical relationship:

$$P = (S / V) (1 - Q)$$

We are now ready to examine what happens to the rate of profit under varying organic compositions of capital.

In order to expand his productive forces and increase productivity, the capitalist introduces machinery and equipment into the production process. Since heavily-mechanized industries tend to be capital-intensive rather than labor-intensive, the capital invested in machinery tends to increase much more quickly than that invested in labor. The numeric value of Q reflects this increasing mechanization, and rises. For example, if we assume a value of 40 for V and insert amounts for C of 100, 120 and 200, we get for Q:

$$Q = 100 / 100 + 40 = 100 / 140 = 0.71$$
$$Q = 120 / 120 + 40 = 120 / 160 = 0.75$$

$$Q = 200 / 200 + 40 = 200 / 240 = 0.83$$

As the value of Q rises, the rate of profit must fall, assuming that the rate of surplus value remains the same. Assuming a steady value of 20 for S, we obtain for the rate of profit:

$$P = (20 / 40) (1 - 0.71) = 0.145$$
$$P = (20 / 40) (1 - 0.83) = 0.082$$

Thus, when the capitalist uses increased machinery and mechanization, and invests a higher proportion of his capital in this area, his rate of profit falls accordingly. This should be obvious—the more expensive the machinery and equipment he uses, the more money he must spend in order to produce the same amount of surplus value with it.

We have assumed, however, that the surplus value which is produced is the same for varying rates of Q. This, of course, is an unrealistic assumption, since the capitalist will not invest in new machinery unless by doing so he can increase the productivity of his workers enough to offset the higher costs. If we assume that the new machinery increases the value of S from 20 to 40, we get a new profit rate of:

$$P = (40 / 40) (1 - 0.83) = 0.17$$

The introduction of new machinery, instead of lowering the rate of profit, has now doubled it.

It is thus apparent that the increasing mechanization of the productive process cannot by itself lead to a tendency for the profit rate to fall. However, the increasing productivity brought about by the process of mechanization is the root cause of the overproduction crisis, which lowers profit levels by reducing the realization of surplus value.

There is also another process which tends to lower the profit rates in the capitalist economy. Since a worker is, in the capitalist system, a commodity like any other, its market price (in the form of wages and compensations) is subject to the same market process of "social necessity" as any other commodity. As labor-saving machinery is introduced at swifter and swifter rates, large numbers of workers find that their labor power is no longer needed by the capitalists. In other words, a portion of the labor force finds itself to be "socially unnecessary", and the price of labor power (wages) tends to fall.

As profits thus expand and are reinvested into new productive ability, the demand for labor power once again rises, and in practice, during periods of economic growth, the demand for new labor power tends to outpace the number of workers who are idled due to labor-saving machinery. As a result, the demand for labor tends to be higher than the available supply, and wages are forced up as capitalists bid against each other for the increasingly scarce work force.

This steady rise in wages, however, produces a corresponding decline in the profit rate, and this decline will take place faster than the capitalist can counter it by introducing labor-saving machinery. Thus, the capitalist must still spend more capital in order to make a profit, but now his rising costs are in the area of variable capital or wages rather than in constant capital or machinery.

The capitalist is thus faced with an insoluble contradiction, as periods of economic expansion contain within them the seeds of their own demise. As expanding productive forces use up the available reserve of workers, the price of labor power (wages) is driven up. And, as the level of wages rises, that of profits falls.

The inescapable result is recession, in which profits fall below an acceptable level, reinvestment of capital is reduced, and the economic expansion slows and then reverses. As production is cut back, workers are laid off to once again produce an idle reserve of labor power, and wages fall.

As wages fall, it once again becomes profitable to reinvest in production, and the economy begins to expand once again. The cycle starts all over again.

This is the essence of the capitalist "business cycle", the periodic pattern of boom and bust. These cycles of expansion and recession, it can now be seen, are not the results of incompetence or incorrect decisions made by business or government leaders; they are an integral and intrinsic part of the capitalist mode of production and cannot, within the framework of capitalism, be either fixed or avoided.

In modern monopoly capitalism, the twin trends of overproduction and cyclical profit rates tend to aggravate and reinforce each other. To counter the rising costs of labor, the capitalist introduces labor-saving machinery, and thus eliminates a large number of workers. This, however, produces another awkward problem—eliminating wage income for workers at the same time reduces the market for the capitalist's commodities, by reducing disposable income and decreasing demand. The problem is best illustrated by a story (perhaps apocryphal) which is told about United Auto Workers President Walter Reuther. One day, it seems, the Ford Motor Company decided to replace all of the workers on an assembly line with robots, and invited Reuther to tour the facility. As they walked along the row of clattering machines, a Ford executive remarked, "Well, Walter, how are you going to be able to get these robots to go out on strike?" Reuther, after a moment, promptly replied, "Well, sir, how are you going to get these robots to buy Fords?"

Thus, despite falling wages levels, it is still not profitable to reinvest in increased productive ability. The economic expansion which had always followed the recession is now uncertain, and the monopolist economy tends to degenerate into a continuous state of idleness, unemployment and stagnation.

The only long-term way out of this lethal situation lies in the development of overseas markets to absorb the monopolist's productive ability and ease the demand crunch, and this seems to be the direction most monopolists have chosen. This, however, will present an entirely new set of problems. Up to this point, we have limited our economic analysis to the industrialized monopolist nations. Now, in order to understand the full picture, we must turn to the non-industrialized economic neo-colonies.

SIX: The Rise of the Leninist Mode of Production

By the time that monopoly capitalism was beginning to arise in the industrialized nations, the world had already been divided into "developed" and "undeveloped" spheres. In the former, the rise of the capitalist bourgeoisie led to the introduction of competitive capitalism and thence to monopoly capitalism. These nations were industrialized and featured a large output of consumer-oriented commodities. Manufacturing and industry were the major sources of wealth.

In the so-called "Third World" nations, however, the situation was completely different. In these nations, the bourgeoisie had never risen to power, and the ancient feudal traditions had never been broken. In countries such as China, Russia, the African nations and Latin America, economic conditions remained essentially feudalist in nature. Feudal aristocrats ruled under various names and titles, and the source of wealth in these agrarian nations was land. Wealthy landowners stood at the top of the economic ladder, and the masses of serfs and agrarian peasants labored to pay their rents and make a living. To all intents and purposes, economic life had not changed much in these areas for the past thousand years.

The student of economic history is therefore forced to ask why these economies had not taken the direction demonstrated in Europe; that is, how was the feudal system able to continue and dominate the economy in these areas? To begin to answer this question, we must take another look at the rise of the European bourgeoisie.

As the bourgeoisie began to rise in importance during the Middle Ages, the economic circumstances of their existence led them to seek foreign sources of exotic commodities for sale to the feudal lords. During these quests for new sources of commodities, the European bourgeoisie first made contact with the peoples of Africa, Asia and, later, the Americas. These traders exchanged European commodities for the native goods they wanted, then sold these native goods in their own home country.

As a result of this commercial trade, sections of the native populations left the feudal landholdings and, like the European artisans, began to make their living by mediating trade between the Europeans and the non-Europeans. In China and the Far East, these merchant-middlemen were known as compradors, and this term has come to be applied to the class of people who perform these functions in all of the feudal nations.

As it did in Europe, this commercial relationship led to the monetarization of the economy and the transformation of the serf-landlord relationship. In order to obtain money for exchange with the Europeans, the native feudal aristocracy began to turn their land from food production to the production of those exchange goods the Europeans wanted, such as silk, tea or spices. In addition, the traditional feudal "tax in kind" was replaced by a monetary rent.

The results profoundly changed the economic structure. From the traditional serf-lord relationship, the basis of the economy was transformed into a landlord-peasant relationship.

While the exchange arrangement set up between Europe and the non-industrialized countries brought benefits to both, these benefits were greatly lopsided in favor of the Europeans. With their greater capital resources and their more highly developed methods of commerce, the European bourgeoisie came to dominate the economy of the native countries. They were able to extract large amounts of exotic trade goods (which could be sold in Europe at huge profits) and also to provide European commodities to the natives at an equally large profit.

As the feudal monarchy and the bourgeoisie entered the stage of mercantilism, increasingly stronger steps were taken to safeguard and expand this lucrative trade arrangement. At the point of a musket, European armies overran huge areas of native lands, imposing control over these "colonies". Some (such as Latin America and parts of Africa) were conquered by direct military force and were ruled directly by European military governors. Others, such as China and Russia, were too large or too strong to be conquered, but were controlled by co-opting the feudal monarch (the Emperor and the Tsar). Soon, a vast amount of wealth began to flow from the conquered colonies into the European monarchy's treasury (as well as into the pockets of the bourgeoisie).

By the time the bourgeoisie managed to overthrow the European monarchies and establish their own regimes, they had established military, political and economic control over vast areas of native territory. The Spanish and Portuguese held most of Latin America, the French and British divided up North America, the Italians and Germans held most of Africa, and Asia was held piecemeal by virtually all of the capitalist powers. Using their superior economic resources and their superior military force, the Europeans grew rich by extracting wealth from their colonies.

After the Industrial Revolution, the emphasis of the capitalist bourgeoisie changed from the procurement of trade commodities to the extraction of cheap raw materials and labor resources from the colonies. Plantations and agricultural enterprises, which yielded huge profits, were also monopolized by the foreigners.

In nearly every instance, each colony was forcibly specialized to produce a single commodity needed by the foreigners. The Spanish colony of Bolivia, for instance, was turned into a huge tin mine, while Indochina was transformed into a vast rubber plantation for the French. Cuba produced sugar for European consumption, Colombia produced coffee, Honduras produced bananas.

Nearly all of the choice land resources in the colonies were seized by the foreigners, who used them to produce their single-commodity export. The rest of the land was occupied by small subsistence farmers, the peasantry, who rented the land which they worked from the wealthy native land-owning aristocracy.

In the manufacturing sector, foreign domination was equally complete. The colony's industrial sector was small, but it was used to produce the cheap raw materials and sub-assemblies needed by the European factory system. While these colonial enterprises employed a number of local workers, the management and capital of these enterprises was always foreign, and the profits from the enterprise were always repatriated back to the imperialist nation.

The native merchant class was eager to begin manufacturing commodities of their own, but found this to be nearly impossible in the face of the near-total domination of the economy by foreign capital. In most instances, the superior productivity of the imperialist's larger capital and the correspondingly lower prices of his commodities meant that the native manufacturer could not compete in his own marketplace.

Thus, the native merchant class was able to survive only by subordinating itself to the foreign imperialists and catching the crumbs which fell from the foreigner's table.

The near-total foreign domination and the consequent lack of a native manufacturing class had far-reaching effects on the economic and social structure of the colony. In Europe, the introduction of the factory system had resulted in the flow of agrarian workers into industry, as landless serfs hired themselves out as laborers. In the colonies, however, where manufacturing was restricted, excess agricultural workers could not be drained off into industry. This in turn forced the population to remain dependent on the agrarian sector, pushing people into bare subsistence farming in a futile attempt to pay high rents and eke out a living.

Such a heavily agrarian population is perfectly suited for exploitation by the monopolists. The enormous pressure put on the land by the lack of industrial development allows the land-owning class to charge usurious rents for postage-stamp farms. At the same time, the dependence of the colony's economy on a single export commodity leaves it vulnerable to the monopolists who control this commodity, allowing foreigners to use their economic leverage to dictate terms of trade and economic relations. Finally, the enormous reserve of labor created by the overcrowded agrarian sector allows the monopolists to keep wages at a bare subsistence level, thus insuring super-profits for the foreigners.

As imperialism and monopoly capitalism began to establish a worldwide network, native colonies began increasing efforts to expel the foreigners and regain control of their own country. These revolts were constantly beaten back by the imperialist's armed forces, but in the end the monopolists realized that, provided they still retained de facto economic control, it would do them no great harm to grant the colonies political independence, and thus allow them to pay for their own government and administration. After World War II, there was a virtual wave of decolonization. In reality, however, the imperialist powers still held the reins, through their economic domination and through the installation of pliant comprador regimes which were tied to the interests of the monopolists.

Thus, the introduction of "decolonization" did virtually nothing to change the structure of the neo-colony. The native landowners still constituted the economic elite. The peasantry still worked the fields and paid outrageous rents to the landlords. The bourgeoisie was still dominated by the foreign monopolists, and the working class still labored for the foreign-owned enterprises, which still repatriated their huge profits. In addition, the middle class or petty bourgeoisie, made up of intellectuals, managers, professionals and small business owners, were immobilized on all sides by the tight web of foreign domination.

When it became apparent that political independence would mean nothing without economic independence, nationalist movements began to arise in the neo-colonies. The comprador state and the landlords, who depended on the protection of the foreigners for their very existence, found themselves under increasing attack.

The neo-colonial bourgeoisie's interests lay in beginning their own manufacturing enterprises to accumulate capital for themselves, but this was prevented by foreign domination of the economy. The interests of the peasantry lay in deposing the landlords and obtaining ownership of their own land, but this was also prevented by the imperialist-backed comprador government. The interests of the workers lay in political and economic freedom so they could organize a labor movement to improve their conditions, but this was impossible. And, finally, the petty bourgeoisie wanted a chance to depose the foreign-backed government and install a new economic regime beneficial to it. Only the landlords, along with those sections of the bourgeoisie who were totally immersed in the monopolist economy, supported the imperialist domination—they had nothing to lose under it and everything to gain with it.

Economic domination by the foreigners meant that the native industrial bourgeoisie and the working class were embryonic at best, and in many neo-colonies they were virtually non-existent. In practice, this left the peasants to form the anti-imperialist nationalist forces.

The class struggle dynamics of the neo-colony are clear. On one side are the land-owning class and the state, which are supported and propped up by the imperialists. On the other side is the petty bourgeoisie, the peasantry and the fledgling working class. The bourgeoisie is divided, with one part supporting the privileges it gains under imperialist protection and another part wishing to overthrow the foreigners and establish their own regime. Thus, nationalist expressions in the neo-colonies are partly anti-feudal and partly anti-imperialist.

Economic stresses in the neo-colony also inevitably lead to revolutionary pressures. The tiny "postage stamp" farms cannot be worked efficiently with modern machinery, and the peasants could not afford to purchase such equipment even if the foreign-dominated manufacturing sector would produce it. As a result, food production slowly lags behind population growth, leading to widespread poverty.

Obviously, to improve agrarian output and feed the population, the economy must invest resources into industry to produce agricultural equipment. However, since the imperialist-dominated economy is directed towards the needs of the monopolists, not the neo-colony, this will seldom occur under the existing system.

The only solution is the removal of imperialist domination and the assumption of economic control by the indigenous people, in order to meet their own needs. Thus, economic necessity forces the neo-colonies to attempt to wrest control of their own economic resources through a nationalist rebellion. Since the imperialists fight to protect their comprador clients, and since peaceful struggle is limited by the existing social structures, these nationalist rebellions invariably take the form of armed "wars of national liberation" to free the economy from the grip of the monopolists.

In Europe and North America, the introduction of machinery into agriculture took place during the Industrial Revolution. This huge investment of capital could not, however, take place until the existing feudal social relationships were broken by the bourgeoisie, which was supported in this task by the peasantry and the rising working class. In the neo-colonies, though, the bourgeoisie is weak and divided, and does not have the economic or political power to lead and carry out an anti-feudal and anti-imperialist revolution. In the absence of a developed bourgeoisie, the task of directing the anti-feudal rebellion and of constructing a new economic system falls to the petty bourgeoisie, allied with the peasantry and the working class.

To succeed in this task, the petty bourgeoisie must be anti-imperialist in its outlook, it has to advocate rapid industrialization and mechanization, it has to have an anti-feudal and anti-bourgeois ideology, and it has to have the support of the peasants and, to a lesser extent, the workers. In 1917, a political party with all of these characteristics deposed the Russian Tsar and seized power.

SEVEN: The Basis of Leninism

When the Bolsheviks came to power in Russia in 1917, they found themselves to be in a unique position. They were the first neo-colony to free themselves from imperialist control in the economic sphere as well as the political. And, as a consequence of this, the new Soviet state was the first ascension to power of the petty bourgeoisie as a class. Despite the Leninist claim that the party represents the interests of the working class, the Russian and all other Leninist revolutions were in fact made by the peasantry, led by the petty bourgeoisie.

Since the petty bourgeoisie had never before managed to attain state power as a class, the Leninists were left to face the awesome task of rebuilding Russia's shattered economy with no historical model to base themselves on; no "petty bourgeois mode of production" had ever existed before. It thus fell to the Leninists to discover, through trial and error, how a petty bourgeois economic order would function.

The primary task faced by the new Leninist state was the immediate buildup of industrial output. This buildup was vital to allow the growth of agricultural productivity so the new nation would be able to feed itself. The hostility of the imperialist monopolists to the new nation, moreover, as demonstrated by their military attempts to overthrow the Leninists and re-establish a pliant comprador state, gave the petty bourgeoisie an additional incentive to industrialize rapidly—they needed to increase military production and arm the nation against foreign intervention.

The immediate task of the Leninist state was to guarantee its economic independence from the imperialists. In order to break the feudal/monopolist hold on the economy, the first act of the Leninist state was to nationalize the Tsarist landholdings and expropriate the lands of the feudal nobility, and to take over all of the foreign-owned heavy industry in Russia. This, at one stroke, placed nearly all of the nation's economic resources under native control and effectively shut out the foreign monopolists. The Leninist state was now ready to face the problems presented by its economic independence.

In order to expand the ability of the agrarian sector to produce food, the ex-colony had to find capital to invest in the industrial sector of the economy, as well as a method of freeing surplus agrarian labor for employment in manufacturing. In Europe, this had been done through the gradual development of the capitalist market system, which prodded the serfs and rural peasants from the land to the cities. This process had, however, taken decades or centuries, and the ex-colony, if it was to survive as an independent economy, did not have the time to wait for such a gradual market-spurred growth. In order to produce rapid industrial expansion, the Leninist ex-colony would have no alternative but to resort to a non-market method of growth.

This had already begun when the Leninists nationalized the feudal and imperialist assets and placed them under state control. The swiftest way to expand the economy's production capability was to invest resources in this sector under the direction of the state. To do this effectively, however, it would be necessary for the state to assume direct control over industry and over investments, and this flow of investment had to be carefully mapped out beforehand to prevent duplication of effort and other wasted resources. In this manner, the need to rapidly expand productive ability forced the Leninists to adopt the expedient of the state-planned economy.

In other words, the Leninist state found itself playing the role of investing and accumulating capital, or producing and appropriating surplus value for investment in the expansion of productive capacity. In the absence of an existing surplus-producing manufacturing sector, and in the absence of the possibility of borrowing or importing capital from the foreign monopolists, the surplus needed for industrial growth could only come from the agrarian sector.

The Leninists therefore had to find a reliable and efficient method of transferring a surplus from the agrarian sector of the economy to the tiny industrial sector. Under the initial policy of "War Communism", the state attempted to set the prices of manufactured goods above their value, thus obtaining a surplus profit from all of the manufactured goods sold to the peasantry. The peasantry, however, responded by withholding grain and other agricultural products rather than trading them for inflated industrial prices.

Under the New Economic Policy, therefore, the state attempted to use low prices on industrial goods to entice the peasantry into producing and selling more agrarian products. This, however, was greatly favorable to the peasants and provided no way for the state to obtain the necessary agrarian surplus.

When all of these various attempts to use the market process failed to produce the needed surplus, Stalin solved the quandary in a practical, if brutal, manner. It was decided by the Leninists that the peasantry would no longer be enticed to produce a surplus for re-investment in industry—they would simply be coerced into producing a surplus which would then be forcibly expropriated by the state.

The system imposed by Stalin is still in effect, in various forms, in all of the remaining Leninist countries. Under this scheme, the peasants were forcibly gathered into large "collective farms", which were then provided with what machinery was available from the industrial sector to increase production. To extract an investable surplus from the collectives, the state set a quota of agricultural output which was provided to the state at prices below value. Any output over quota was divided up between the members of the collective. At first, the mandatory state quota was taken as a "tax in kind". This was later altered to a monetary tax.

This relationship is, of course, essentially feudal in nature, with the state directly appropriating a portion of the peasant's labor. In this manner, the Leninists obtained the surplus they needed for reinvestment into industrial expansion.

The interests of the state and the peasantry are, in the Leninist system, wholly irreconcilable. The Leninist state's interests lie in appropriating an ever-increasing portion of agrarian output. The interests of the peasantry are to own their own land and thus to keep their production for themselves. Thus, the Leninist state is forced to combat the interests of the peasantry with force; the Leninists must use purely repressive methods to safeguard their position of domination.

Originally, industrialization is seen as a means to expand agrarian output. If the ex-colony is to maintain its economic independence, however, it must also strive to be as completely self-sufficient, economically, as possible, and must develop a productive capacity large enough to meet its own internal needs. This must take the form of a massive growth of production-sector commodities—in effect, an Industrial Revolution. Since investment in consumer-oriented commodities means a correspondingly lower investment in production-oriented goods, the Leninists are forced, in order to industrialize as rapidly as possible, to lower the output of consumer goods. Consumer commodity production is restricted to the lowest level necessary to bring about bare consumer subsistence and political stability.

Since the resulting shortages and rationing provoke hostility among the peasants and the workers, the Leninist state is once again forced to resort to a repressive network of police and military forces to protect its position of privileged access to scarce consumer goods.

In China under Mao Zedong, where the peasantry was a much larger and more powerful force than in Russia, the immediate introduction of this Leninist strategy was politically impossible, and would have provoked opposition and internal conflict. Mao, therefore, attempted to placate the peasantry by reducing the expropriation of the agrarian surplus and by producing consumer commodities at the expense of heavy industry.

As a result of the Maoist peasant-oriented strategy, however, economic growth in China has never approached the level achieved by the Soviet Union. To the extent that investment in the production-goods sector of the economy is less than total, the growth of productive ability is slowed and economic independence takes that much longer. Thus, although factions within the Leninist countries may argue over questions of "market methods vs. planned methods" or "consumer goods vs. industrial goods" or "agrarian investment vs. industrial investment", economic necessity will force them to adopt the "planned rapid industrialization" program as the only way to maintain economic independence.

In order to plan effectively for the swiftest possible industrial growth, it is necessary for the Leninist state to concentrate all economic resources in its hands. This is accomplished by the simple expedient of nationalizing the entire production process, in essence putting the entire economy under government ownership. Since the government is made up by a petty bourgeois bureaucracy, Leninist state ownership of industry is essentially petty bourgeois ownership of industry. While in the monopolist economy the bourgeoisie controls the means of production and uses the state to safeguard its position, in the Leninist mode of production the petty bourgeoisie uses the state as the means of controlling the means of production. Rather than simply *protecting* the ruling class, the Leninist bureaucracy actually *is* the ruling class.

We would expect, in Marxian terms, that this new economic system would be organized so as to allow those who control the means of production to make their living by extracting surplus value from the economy, as the feudal lord makes his living by expropriating the labor of the serf and the bourgeois capitalist class makes its living by extracting unpaid labor from the working class. Study of the Leninist economic system shows this to be true. This expropriation takes place through the mechanism of the Leninist pricing system.

In the non-market Leninist system, prices are not determined by "social necessity" in the marketplace, but are set solely by government fiat. A commodity "costs" such and such a price and the worker is paid such and such a wage because that is what the state planners have decided the price and wage should be. Therefore, state planners are free to set wages and prices in such a way as to create as much surplus as they wish.

Under War Communism, prices were set high so as to generate a higher "profit" for the state when they were sold. This, however, led the agrarian farmers to simply withhold their stocks of grain rather than trading them on unfavorable terms. The next alternative, the NEP, lowered industrial prices and wages so as to try to entice more output from the peasantry. This, however, benefited the peasantry more than the state.

Once forced collectivization took place, however, the ability of the peasantry to withhold production was ended, and the price system evolved into a combination of these two strategies. Now, industrial prices could be set high to generate a large surplus, but wages could also at the same time be kept low to increase this surplus.

The relationship between the worker and the state, therefore, is similar to the basic formula M-C-M', where the state invests a certain amount of money M (which it extracted from the agrarian sector) and uses it to produce a commodity C which is then sold at a price which returns more money to the state. The Leninist state thus acts as an owner of capital, as a capitalist; and, since the state is the only producer in the economy, as a monopoly capitalist. The Leninist system can be viewed as a sort of "state capitalist" system.

In the capitalist system, the production of surplus value is a function of producing commodities for less than their value and then selling them at their full value. Under monopolist conditions, commodities can be produced for less than their value and then sold for more than their value, thus producing super-profits. In the Leninist system, there is no market to influence the final price of commodities. The state is a true monopolist and can set whatever price it wishes. And, since the state sets the wages as well, it can directly determine the amount of surplus value it will receive.

In capitalism, the wages paid to the workers cannot fall below the minimum labor value needed by the worker to live. In Leninist state capitalism, however, this labor value itself can be predetermined, by setting a wage scale and then manipulating prices to cheapen this wage. The minimum means of living are sold at prices which are themselves set by the state. Thus, the Leninist state is able to set the prices of the worker's means of living at artificially low levels, lowering the worker's labor value and allowing the state to extract even more surplus value.

This surplus can then be increased even further by simply raising the price received for the commodity which is produced. In practice, it is easier (both administratively and politically) for the state to influence its profit levels by changing prices rather than wage levels.

The profit levels appropriated by the state are thus determined by the wage levels chosen for the economy and by the price level chosen for each commodity. For example, let us assume that it costs the Leninist state 3 rubles in depreciated machinery and 5 rubles in wages to produce a commodity, and that the state wishes a surplus value of 75%. To obtain this profit level, the state must set its price for this commodity at 32 rubles. The extra 24 rubles, which are not related to the costs of production, go directly to the state, much as an assessment or tax would. In fact, this added quantity is known as the "turnover tax", and the prices of all goods sold in the Soviet Union carried it, as well as an additional state tax known as the "deduction from profits tax". Also, the enterprise itself was allowed to tack on a small profit to be used for reinvestment into its own operations.

The total surplus for the commodity is thus:

$$S = T + D + P$$

where T is the turnover tax, D is the deduction from profits tax and P is the enterprise's profit for reinvestment. Of these, T and D go directly to the state, where they are appropriated as surplus value.

The Leninist petty bourgeoisie (organized as the state) thus makes its living by appropriating the surplus value created by the workers and peasants. The total value of T plus D is allocated at the discretion of the state planning apparatus. Of this amount, a portion goes for reinvestment into expanded productive ability. A portion, however, is used for the salaries, bonuses and other perks enjoyed by the apparatchiks and government officials. By virtue of its role as state-capitalist owner of the means of production, the petty bourgeois bureaucracy is able to force others to produce its living for it.

In its role as ruling class, the Leninist state exercises the privilege of directing the national economy in the manner that will best serve to protect and expand its interests. The Five Year Plans shift in their emphasis from heavy industry to military output to space exploration to consumer industry as the international and domestic situation demands. State power to control wages is used to selectively raise wages in one industry in order to attract workers, and to lower wages in other industries to encourage workers to move to other areas. Price controls create artificially low prices for essential consumer goods (food, clothing, etc) both to cheapen the value of labor power and to defuse popular resentment at the constant shortages and rationing.

Thus, the basic operation of the Soviet state is purely exploitative. The state bureaucracy extracts surplus value from the agrarian sector in a semi-feudal relationship, and directs this investment towards heavy industry. And, as a state capitalist, the bureaucracy extracts surplus value through wage and price control, and uses this surplus value for itself.

The class dynamics of the Leninist state are thus inherently hostile. The petty bourgeoisie rules by virtue of its control of the state planning apparatus, which sets economic goals and priorities. The agrarian sector is ruthlessly exploited by the state bureaucracy, and the workers receive artificially low wages and live in an economy of artificial poverty and shortages.

These intra-national conflicts are compounded by international pressures. In order to continually feed the expanding heavy-industrial program, the Leninist state must have sources of labor and raw materials, as well as constant sources of new investable surplus. The lack of investment in the agrarian sector limits the amount of resources which can be diverted from it to the industrial program, and quickly leads to a "labor crunch" in the Leninist economy. This in turn slows the rate of industrial growth.

The solution to this problem lies in extra-national expansion in a search for new labor sources. The Leninist state is therefore, like the monopolists, driven by economic pressures into an expansionistic foreign policy, and is driven to seize and hold its own economic colonies. After installing a pliant comprador state, the Leninist imperialists impose heavily lopsided trade agreements and economic alliances which are of benefit to the Leninist economy. In the captive nations of Eastern Europe, for instance, the Soviets used the Comecon economic "alliance" to utilize native labor and resources to produce subassemblies which were shipped back to Russia, assembled there and then sold back to the natives at inflated prices. In essence, the Soviet Union used the Comecon structure, propped up by the Warsaw Pact military network, to siphon resources from Eastern Europe for investment in the Soviet economy.

Thus, in the international arena, the inherent expansionism of the Leninist system makes it vulnerable to many of the same stresses which plague international monopoly capitalism. The Leninist system itself, moreover, has its own internal economic stresses which steadily weaken and undermine it.

EIGHT: Leninist Contradictions

The inherent expansionism of the Leninist system drives it to overrun and conquer colonies abroad, just as the expansionistic pressures of the monopoly capitalists force them to do the same. The result is increased international conflicts and tensions over the exploitation of neo-colonies.

The Soviet Union, the only Leninist state so far to reach this expansionistic phase, dominated the neo-colonies of Eastern Europe, Southeast Asia, parts of Africa and Cuba. These neo-colonies served as sources of investable surplus for the Soviet industrialization program.

This political, economic and military domination by the Soviets, however, naturally produced in the neo-colonies a desire to be rid of the foreigners. This was true not only in neo-colonies such as Poland, Czechoslovakia and East Germany, but also in the "internal colonies", the non-Russian Federated

Republics of Georgia, Latvia, Uzbekistan, Kazakhstan and Lithuania. A constant struggle rages between the Soviet Union, which needs the economic colonies for its economic development, and the neo-colonies, who desire to be free of foreign domination and to control their own economic resources. This struggle is held in check by the Soviet military.

A handful of these nations may possess sufficient resources to gain economic as well as political independence from Soviet domination. Nations such as Poland or Czechoslovakia, which have withdrawn from the Soviet orbit, may be able, if they do not fall under the domination of the industrialized monopolists, to apply the same principles of planned economic growth and emerge as fully independent industrial economies. This, in essence, would be a "Leninist" neo-colonial revolt directed against a Leninist imperialist power. This is what happened in China during the Sino-Soviet split in the 1960's.

Within the framework of the Leninist system itself, however, there are internal contradictions and stresses which will weaken and eventually destroy it. One of these contradictions may be termed the tendency towards the overproduction of production-goods.

The aim of the Leninist state is to expand the production-goods and heavy-industrial sector to the most rapid extent possible. In the early stages of the system, this is carried out by transferring surplus which is extracted from the agrarian sector. Once the maximum amount of resources have been siphoned from the agricultural sector, however, new sources of investment and labor must be found. Therefore, the tendency is for the extraction of surplus through the sale of state-produced commodities to play an increasingly more prominent role in the Soviet economy.

One method of doing this would be to simply sell production goods themselves at a profit, to produce a surplus for more capital investment. This is done to a certain extent by the sale of equipment and machinery abroad by the Soviet Union. It is in the interests of the Soviet government, however, to have as much productive ability as possible remain inside the country, in order to avoid economic dependence on foreign-made commodities.

Soviet arms sales to client states and would-be client states also generate huge profits and sources of investment, and have the additional benefit of reinforcing the Soviet grip on their neo-colonies. However, the market for military products cannot be expanded to indefinite levels, and cannot provide a steady source of investable income.

The final alternative is to produce and sell consumer commodities at a profit. Profits on consumer goods flow to the state in the form of turnover taxes and provide a steady source of funds for the industrialization effort. However, the priority which is given to the production sector over the consumer sector reduces the amount of commodities which are available, and the low wages paid to Leninist consumers tends to limit this option as well.

The lopsided Leninist investment program produces disproportion between the production sector and the consumer sector. The equilibrium relationship between these sectors is the same as that in a monopoly capitalist economy, that is:

$$Vp + (Sp1 + Sp3) = Ck + Sk2$$

In other words, the consumptive ability of the productive sector must be matched by the productive ability of the consumer sector.

In the Leninist system, however, economic realities demand that investments be maximized in the productive sector at the expense of the consumer sector. These investments in the value of P tend to increase the values of Vp (wages paid to workers in the production sector), Sp3 (surplus which is invested in production employee wages) and Sp1 (surplus from the production sector which goes towards consumption by the state bureaucrats) at rates which are higher than increases in

Ck (investment in consumer sector constant capital) and Sk2 (surplus invested in consumer constant capital). This, in effect, tends to produce the inequality:

$$Vp + (Sp1 + Sp3) > Ck + Sk2$$

In other words, consumptive ability (demand) in the production sector grows faster than it can be fulfilled by the productive ability (supply) of the consumer sector. One could say that production capacity is being overproduced, or that consumer capacity is being underproduced.

In either case, the productive capacity produced by the capital-goods sector is not absorbed by the consumer sector rapidly enough to offset the increased demand for consumer goods which its expansion creates. Since this productive capacity is not effectively utilized, it is in effect idled. Underdevelopment of the Leninist consumer sector thus has the effect of saddling the economy with sluggishness and loss of growth.

The solution for the problem is fairly obvious; the Leninist state must expand consumer production in order to produce an outlet for its productive capacity. It is in this requirement, however, that another problem arises—the Leninist system is not well-suited for the production of consumer commodities.

The development of "basic industry" poses no problem for the Leninist centralized command system. Indeed, this system has proven to be the most rapid way to develop and expand heavy industries and productive capacity. However, the needs of a consumer economy are not integrated well into the Leninist command structure.

The ponderous central planning commission (GOSPLAN) is at a considerable distance from the eventual consumption of its commodities. Any problems or possibilities which arise must penetrate several layers of bureaucracy before reaching the central planners who have the authority to respond to these changes. In an expanding economy, no central apparatus has the ability to receive and process the countless bits of information which must be taken into account in economic decisions. It becomes an impossible task for the central planning body, once a basic level of industrialization is reached, to keep in touch with all of the changing needs of the economy.

The only solution to this problem is to decentralize economic control by making the lower levels of the economic structure more autonomous and flexible, allowing them to quickly respond to local circumstances without waiting for instructions from the ponderous economic bureaucracy. Within the confines of the Soviet system, this can only take place in the form of expanding the portion of surplus which is made available to the enterprise managers for reinvestment, and giving the managers more latitude in economic decisions.

This process has been introduced several times in Soviet history, beginning with the Liberman economic reforms of the 1960's. Its most recent incarnation was Gorbachev's plans for perestroika, or "restructuring". Perestroika had as its aim an increased ability for enterprise managers to utilize their resources to make and carry out economic decisions at a local level, which the central planning apparatus was unable to do effectively.

Perestroika thus had the intended effect of placing more and more of the Soviet enterprise's surplus value under the direct control of the managers, who were responsible for reinvesting it in such a way as to expand the surplus it generated. In other words, the enterprise manager takes on the role of a controller of capital—of a capitalist—with the goal of maximizing the surplus value created by his investments. This has the effect of creating a neo-bourgeois class among the managers, whose economic interests grow to be more and more opposed to those of the Leninist state.

This tendency is reinforced by the growing need, under perestroika, to use profit as a criteria in planning and investment. In the beginning of the Leninist mode of production, the sole objective of the planning apparatus is simply to expand output as rapidly as possible. Early Leninist planning is concerned solely with putting together the nation's meager natural resources of land, labor and available raw materials to produce maximum output, with no regard for how these resources could be used efficiently. Absolute production output was the determining bottom line.

As the economy grows, however, these resources (particularly labor) become more limited. The lack of investment in agricultural productivity means that the Leninist state has run out of surplus agrarian workers to transfer to the industrial sector, and the Leninist nations experience a severe labor shortage.

In the light of these realities, Leninist planners must now seek to increase growth with the most efficient use possible of scarce resources. In other words. the state must maximize output with the minimum use of capital and resources. Thus, surplus must be considered in proportion to the capital which is used to generate it, or:

$$S \, / \, V + C$$

This proportion is nothing more than P, the capitalist rate of profit.

The position of the Soviet factory manager thus grows closer to M-C-M', in which the manager takes the surplus which the state allows him to keep, invests it in commodity production, and receives a larger surplus, a portion of which he is allowed to keep and reinvest.

In order to perform this task effectively, the enterprise manager must seek the ability to set wages, prices and other factors in order to respond to local conditions and maximize surplus value. These powers are, however, the prerogative of the state planning apparatus, which uses them to appropriate surplus value for the Leninist bureaucrats. Thus, the inherent trends within the Leninist system produce growing class conflict between the petty bourgeois ruling class and the growing neo-capitalist enterprise managers.

Another problem within the central planning apparatus is that of disproportionality. The centralized planning system lacks the resources to expand every sphere of the economy at once. As a result, it concentrates what resources it has into a few areas which are important for economic or political reasons—the expansion of heavy industry, increased consumer production, the space program, or military production.

Within each particular Five Year Plan, a particular industry or economic sector is emphasized and pushed while the others are allowed to lag for lack of resources. Eventually, however, these lagging sectors produce shortages and bottlenecks which interrupt growth, and these must be dealt with in subsequent Five Year Plans—at the expense of still other sectors. The Leninist planning system degenerates into a constant attempt to patch up weak links and eliminate bottlenecks.

The only solution to this problem lies in the simultaneous development of all sectors of the economy, so that no one sector is able to outrun the others. This simultaneous development can only take place through the constant interaction of the differing sectors, so that the development of any one is dependent on the development of the rest.

As these economic sectors interact, however, their increasing autonomy is at odds with the central planning apparatus, which finds itself increasingly useless. The rudiments of a market-oriented exchange system begin to rise as individual enterprises deal with each other to produce the resources, materials and capital necessary to fulfill their individual economic goals.

The inexorable decentralization of the Leninist economy finds itself in conflict with the centralized petty bourgeois state in every sphere. The rising neo-capitalist enterprise managers will begin to assert their economic autonomy, and will come to view the appropriation of portions of their surplus by the state as an intolerable burden. In the agrarian sector, capitalist relations assert themselves in the form of a class conflict between rural workers and the semi-feudal state relations. The Leninist state's repressive apparatus is less and less able to contain the growing class conflicts, and the neo-capitalist classes come to view the Leninist system as a naked mechanism for extracting surplus for the benefit of the state bureaucrats. Subjective and objective conditions combine to weaken the Leninist state and destroy it from within.

At this point, the reader may note that at no time in our analysis of the Leninist system did we introduce the influence of the state's "Marxist" or "Communist" ideology, which economists in the West have assumed to play a vital role in the structure and operation of the Soviet Union. The reason for this omission is clear—the Leninist state's ideological claims have no relation to its structures and actions, any more than the monopoly capitalist's actions have anything to do with the "democracy" and "freedom" which he so loudly declares. The theory and practice of the Leninist states do not have their source in Marxism or in Communism; they are inevitable consequences of the neo-colony's economic conditions and historical legacy. It is in the economics of the Leninist state that we find the reasons for its downfall, not in its politics or ideology.

NINE: The Future of Leninism

As we have seen, the development of the Leninist state eventually leads to a growing class conflict between the petty bourgeois state-capitalists who control the means of production and the neo-capitalist classes which develop within this structure. This class struggle can only be hostile in nature, producing ever-stronger economic crises and faction fights within the existing political and economic structures. This conflict is exacerbated by the constant attempts of the neo-colonies to end their domination by the Soviet state. The interests of the neo-colonies and the neo-capitalists are the same; the overthrow of the Leninist state.

Eventually, the subjective and objective conditions meet, and the Leninist state falls to combined pressures from within and without. The now-victorious neo-capitalist enterprise managers will then restructure the state and the economy to form a new monopoly-capitalist state.

At the time of this writing, only the Soviet Union and its satellites, among the Leninist states, has reached a sufficient level of economic development so as to produce the crises and stresses of a fully-matured Leninist system. Gorbachev's *perestroika* was a vain attempt to solve the internal contradictions which were crippling the Leninist system, by granting the decentralization which was demanded by circumstances, but attempting to keep this decentralization within limits that would not harm the Soviet state. That effort was doomed to failure.

Since, however, the Leninist mode of production is suited so well almost exclusively to the needs of an ex-colonial economy, we might ask the question, will every neo-colony in the world undergo a period of Leninist industrialization and expansion? The answer to this question must be "No".

It should be apparent that, in order for a nation to achieve economic independence (through whatever means), it is necessary for this economy to possess or have access to sufficient resources to enable it to build an independent economy, one that is not dependent for vital resources on imperialist nations. Small nations which possess few resources are incapable of building a self-sufficient economy, since they will always be dependent on commercial relations with other countries. In a world of monopoly imperialism, these relations will always be lopsided. These small nations will remain neo-colonies.

Thus, successful Leninist industrial development is possible only in those neo-colonies which possess sufficient resources for an independent economy, in which the only thing holding back such a development is the crushing oppression of imperialism. Only a handful of neo-colonies have this capacity. If these nations are to achieve economic independence, they must take the "China Road" by closing themselves off to dependence upon either the monopoly capitalists or the Leninist imperialists.

Other neo-colonies in which anti-feudal and anti-imperialist revolutions are successful will be unable to maintain their economic independence. These smaller nations have insufficient resources for internal development and are locked into dependence upon one power bloc or another for these resources. They can successfully revolt in order to leave one power bloc for another, but they do not have the ability to develop economic independence.

As the process of the transition to capitalism in the Leninist nations is completed, therefore, the smaller neo-colonies will lack the economic aid and support to enable them to build an independent economy, and no new colonies will be able to fight their way to economic independence. As those nations with the capacity for Leninist growth and development do so, the possibility for successful anti-imperialist revolution fades.

Thus, as the independent Leninist states undergo a transformation to capitalism, the Leninist mode of production will disappear. The global economy will once again consist of rival monopolist blocs who fight amongst themselves over their neo-colonial dominions. The world will once again be sharply divided into a handful of monopolist exploiters and the vast mass of workers. At this stage, the monopolists are subjected ever more severely to their own internal contradictions and crises.

TEN: The Rise of Socialism

In the past few chapters, we have examined the effects which the economic development of monopoly capitalism has had on the development of the neo-colonial countries. To complete this picture, we must now consider the effects which the development of the neo-colonies has had on the monopoly capitalists.

The twin crises of overproduction and falling profits leave the monopolists in a dilemma. In order to avoid the lethal stagnation caused by the overproduction crisis, the monopolists are forced to expand their markets into the neo-colonies as an outlet for their surplus capital. This will increase effective demand and allow the monopolists to escape, at least temporarily, from the ravages of overproduction.

From this point on, we leave the empirical observation of the world and enter the future. Just as Marx ended his study of capitalism with an introduction of the concept of monopoly capital, but was unable to empirically analyze the phenomenon of monopoly capitalism because it had not yet been fully developed at the time he examined it, so must we in our present analysis end our empirical observations with the onset of the capitalist monopoly crisis. We cannot empirically examine the future development of capitalism, but we can nevertheless make some informed guesses about what lies ahead.

Our starting point for these projections is the trend towards the development of consumer markets in the neo-colonies. Since this is the only practical way out of the overproduction problem, we can be fairly certain that this trend will continue.

This "cure" is, however, only temporary. No matter how far the monopolists may be able to expand their markets, the planet is only so big. Once the monopolists have turned the whole globe into their market, they can expand no more. Once again, the capacity to produce will outrun the ability of the world market to absorb these commodities profitably, and the global market will be engulfed in the stagnation and depression which are typical of late monopoly capitalism.

In order to increase their own profits, the monopolists may in desperation resort once again to all-out competition, which will eliminate all but a tiny number of global corporate empires, in essence putting the entire world economy into the hands of a small clique of capital-owners. Nevertheless, this will do nothing to halt the deadly effects of the monopoly crises.

The steady increase in productive capacity acts, slowly, to erode the basic pillars of capitalism by undermining the market system. The capitalist economy is based, in theory at least, on the "scarcity of resources". Since the economy does not possess sufficient productive ability to produce all of the things we would like to have, a mechanism must be found to allocate resources to the most beneficial areas, at the expense of other less-important sectors which go neglected. In the capitalist system, this is done through the interaction of supply and demand in the marketplace. The most important sectors of the economy (as determined by higher demand) attract investments to supply these needs while less-important areas (with lower demand) attract correspondingly fewer resources to meet this supply.

In the capitalist system, people "compete" for scarce resources through the price system. When the supply of a commodity is scarce, Consumer X is willing or able to pay more than Consumer Y in order to obtain it, and the marketplace is capitalism's method of determining this relationship. As potential productive capacity continues to expand, however, the need for this mechanism steadily erodes.

In modern monopoly capitalist countries, humankind has assembled the most awesome and powerful productive capabilities ever before seen. In fact, these economies are capable of turning out so many commodities that they are strapped for a place to get rid of them all. In such an abundant economy, the notion of "scarcity" is a thing of the past; the only scarcity which exists results from the monopolist's attempts to deal with the overproduction problem by idling progressively larger portions of productive capacity. These economies are capable of producing incredible wealth even when functioning at just 60% or 70% of capacity.

In the neo-colonies, commodities are scarce, but this is because their productive capabilities have been deliberately crippled by monopoly capitalism. If the undeveloped productive capacity of the neo-colonies were to be combined with the "excess" un-utilized capacity of the industrialized nations, total human productive ability would be staggering. Such productive capacity would be capable of eliminating material want from the face of the earth forever, and "scarcity" would be an outmoded concept that belonged to our barbaric and undeveloped past.

In these super-abundant economies, the role of marketplace allocation becomes less and less important. Instead of determining whether Consumer X or Consumer Y will obtain this scarce commodity, the super-productive economy is faced with the problem of devising the most efficient way to distribute commodities to both X and Y. Thus, in a post-scarcity economic system, the allocation and distribution of resources is a social process based on need, not a market process based on supply and demand.

Of course, under monopoly capitalism, the full development and utilization of productive abilities is hampered by the monopolists, who are forced by their class interests to cut back on the utilization of productive forces in order to avoid producing more commodities than they can make a profit with. Thus, rather than producing an economy in which full productive ability is utilized for everyone's benefit, monopoly capitalism produces a situation in which productive ability is deliberately stunted and limited to protect the interests of a small minority. As Marx so accurately foresaw, the capitalist system itself becomes a "fetter on production", and must be broken if the full productive abilities of the economy are to be realized.

As capitalism develops, the share of wealth and income which go to the working class tends to become less and less. Despite what some have assumed, Marx never asserted that the working class would become absolutely impoverished in terms of real income. Critics of Marx have pointed out, correctly, that, rather than declining, the standard of living of the working class has steadily grown.

What has become apparent, however, is that the share of wealth which goes to the workers tends to shrink in comparison with the share of wealth that goes to the capitalists. Thus, even when the actual purchasing power of the working class tends to rise over time, that of the capitalists rises even more; no matter how much the workers receive, the bosses receive still more. Thus, even though the working class is not absolutely impoverished, it tends to become more and more relatively impoverished.

As the overproduction tendency forces the monopolists to cut back more and more on productive forces, the ranks of the unemployed grow, pushing more of the working class into idleness and poverty. In the neo-colonies, the population continues to grow poorer and poorer as profits and wealth flow out of the country and into the monopolist's pockets.

The exploited neo-colonies and the growing number of unemployed workers in the imperialist countries thus develop mutual interests. They are both dependent on the full utilization of productive forces to lift them out of relative poverty and stagnation, but this is made impossible by the monopolist's control over the economy. The enormous benefits which would result from the full utilization and equitable distribution of the world's productive ability—virtually wiping out poverty and material want at a stroke—are instead being monopolized by a small handful of private capital-owners. The image of a tiny wealthy elite existing alongside a growing tide of deprivation and want is striking.

Inevitably, the toilers realize that the monopoly capitalists are not at all necessary for the process of production and are, in essence, social parasites. They do not labor to produce anything, they do not manage their own enterprises; instead, they hire others to do this for them. In short, they do nothing to earn their keep, and live solely by forcing others to make their living for them.

These subjective and objective conditions insure that, not only will the monopolist stranglehold on productive forces be smashed, but the capitalist class itself will be smashed. The workers and toilers rise together and destroy capitalist property relationships—the expropriators are themselves expropriated.

The productive forces which have been assembled by monopoly capitalism are seized by the toilers, raised to their full potential and turned towards filling the needs of the global population rather than towards filling the pockets of the monopolist minority. Hunger, material want and poverty are abolished. The socialist mode of production is born.

ELEVEN: Capitalism and Hegemony

The point of view which we have examined so far, which focuses largely on the economic structures of capitalism and imperialism, is the point of view taken by most Leninists. Though the traditional Leninists may disagree on the conclusions to be reached through such an analysis, they accept the basic principle that the economic structures of a society determine the basic dynamics and development of that society.

This Leninist view of Marxian theory is however, incomplete, and cannot describe the capitalist mode of production as a whole. It is incapable of explaining or allowing us to understand the non-economic factors which are an important part of bourgeois reproduction. Leninist theory does not address the process under capitalism of reproducing and fulfilling the various non-economic human needs such as creativity, self-fulfillment and human relationships. When it does treat these things, it treats them as mere commodity relationships which are exploited by the capitalists in order to sell more products.

Leninists ignore the fact that the conflict between the worker and the capitalist is not merely economic, not merely a matter of haggling over wages, profits and surplus value. It is a social conflict as well, with the workers actively fighting for such non-economic goals as creativity, self-expression, enjoyment and decision-making ability.

Traditional Leninism, finally, ignores such non-economic forms of oppression as racism, sexism, heterosexism, nationalism and authoritarianism. Such very real forces, when they are examined at all, are treated by Leninists as simply a "sub-species" of the economic relationships between capitalists and workers.

These limitations in the Leninist outlook are caused by its tendency to view a social mode of production in strictly economic terms, as merely a method by which the necessaries of life are produced and distributed. But, in order to exist, any social mode of production must be capable of reproducing, not only the physical means of existence, but also all of the various social frameworks which make up human society. All modes of production must determine, not only how the needs of life are produced (economics) but also how different members of society relate to each other and to other societies (race, sexual roles, religion, ethnicity, gender, etc.) and the form of the power and authority structures which hold the social framework together (law, police, state, education, etc.). Taken together, all of these various social constructions make up the total mode of production, and determine how any society is able to relate to itself and to its surroundings—how it is able to reproduce its existence.

There is a tendency among critics of existing society to look at these social structures as if one of these social processes were "primary" and the rest were mere reflections of this. Radical feminists, for instance, view all of human history as a function of the relationships between genders, and thus use "sexism" as a lens through which to view human society.

Anarchists see society in terms of power and control, and thus focus their views on the relationships of authority in human societies. African-American, Latino, Native American and other racial or national activists view society in terms of differing ethnic entities, and thus view human development in terms of racial and national relationships.

Traditional Leninists focus on the economic sphere, and view societal development as a function of the interactions of economic classes. Among most Marxists, this point of view is set out in the so-called "base-superstructure" paradigm, which asserts that economic relationships are the "base" from which society springs, and all other relationships (racial, sexual, national) are merely a "superstructure" which is built upon this base in order to preserve and protect it.

Each of these particular outlooks is incomplete and misleading. In a real functioning society of human beings, each of these "sub-systems" interpenetrates with the others, making the dividing lines between them hazy and indistinct. In South Africa, for instance, the social need to institutionalize the apartheid system of racism led to efforts to limit Blacks to certain jobs, to limit their educational opportunities and to limit the amount of income they control. In Northern Ireland, anti-Catholic religious bigotry served to defend nationalist interests brought about by a colonialist occupation.

Of course, the reverse of these relationships is also true, and Leninists may argue that these racial and national systems are deliberate frauds which are perpetrated by the capitalists in order to keep the workers divided and thus protect their profit-making activities. This argument, however, reduces the whole of human society to economics, an abstraction which does not occur in reality. In the real world, all of these social constructions interact to support, defend and reproduce the bourgeois mode of production as a whole, its totality of social relationships, and not merely capitalist profit-making. For instance, white capitalists in the Southern United States viciously and violently resisted efforts at desegregation and integration, despite the very limited impact this had on the economic sphere. No capitalist would lose money if Blacks were allowed to eat at a lunch counter or sit at the front of a bus, yet the capitalists resisted these efforts fiercely. By challenging the bourgeois structures of race and authority, the civil rights movement directly challenged the ability of the bourgeois mode of production to reproduce its social relationships, and thus posed a threat to the entire order.

In every sphere of bourgeois society, these "sub-structures" appear, and interpenetrate to reinforce and reproduce each other. In the workplace, an economic struggle takes place between capitalist and worker over wages and profits. At the same time, an authority struggle rages between employee and employer over decision-making within the workplace, while racial and gender struggles center around equal opportunity, equal pay and decision-making ability. In the universities and educational institutions of bourgeois society, these same struggles occur. Economically, the children of wealthy people receive better educations and are trained to assume roles of authority and leadership. Students from poorer families, on the other hand, receive "vocational training" to prepare them for a place in the capitalist's factories and workplaces, and also learn to accept the authority and discipline of the boss. Women are trained for "girl's" jobs and roles, and sexual and racial roles are strengthened and reinforced by education.

In the nuclear family, some are dependent on the wages and income received by others, and this economic relationship reinforces the authority the wage earner exercises over the rest. Women are assigned definite family roles to play, and men are expected to play quite different roles. Unwritten rules concerning friendships, playmates and marriages reinforce the "socially accepted" relationships between families of different ethnicity, religion or class.

The result of this interconnecting web of social structures is to insure that each and every segment of bourgeois society is conditioned, and required to reproduce the various social relationships which are vital to the preservation and reproduction of the total system. The economic role of wage earner reinforces the dependence of the family on the wage system, and thus reinforces the gender roles of "wife" and "husband". At the same time, the authority of the man over the woman in the home conditions the woman to accept the boss's authority in the workplace, and thus guarantees that the economic exploitation of women can continue. This in turn produces higher profits for the capitalist, and reinforces his position of authority over the wage earner.

We can thus see that, contrary to the assertions of the Leninists, the economic struggle per se is not the only conflict in the bourgeois system, and therefore is not the only struggle which can result in an awareness of oppression and the development of a revolutionary consciousness. Sexism, racism and national oppression can all lead to a revolutionary challenge to the system itself, by challenging the very social relationships through which that system reproduces itself. For example, racial consciousness produced revolutionary ideas among the Black liberation movements of the 1960's and in the South African ANC, while most neo-colonial revolutionaries have been won to their position through awareness of national oppression rather than simple economic exploitation.

Leninists, by arguing that non-economic relationships such as sexism and racism are simply "reflections" of an underlying economic "base", are ignoring the fact that capitalism didn't invent any of these "isms". All of them existed before capitalism was born, and, as recent experiences in the Soviet Union and other Leninist nations have shown, they do not automatically disappear in a non-capitalist economy.

The error of the traditional Leninists lies in the narrowness of their interpretation of the word "economic". By "economic mode of production", the Leninists usually mean simply that system which produces and distributes goods such as food, clothing, and shelter. Marx, however, asserted that, in order to survive, humans must constantly interact with their surroundings, and in order to do this, humans must organize themselves into a society which can carry out this process of interrelation. This society was termed by Marx a "mode of production"; not simply a mode of producing material goods for consumption, but also a mode of producing the ideas, attitudes and social relationships which allowed that human society to exist, expand and reproduce itself. In this sense, the term "mode of production" goes far beyond mere economic activity—it includes all of human society's methods for interacting with itself and with its natural surroundings.

Towards the end of his life, Marx intended to write a series of books, detailing the structure of the total bourgeois "mode of production", and intended to examine the roles of the state, the arts, law and esthetics in the reproduction of bourgeois society. Unfortunately for future Marxists, he lived long enough only to begin the first of this projected series, *Capital*, which dealt exclusively with capitalist economics. Marx never had the opportunity to examine the various non-economic aspects of the bourgeois mode of production.

Thus, a full study of Marxian "economics" must inevitably lead to a study of racism, nationalism, heterosexism, religious bigotry, ageism, authoritarianism, and all of the other methods by which bourgeois society protects and propagates itself. Contrary to the assertions of the Leninists, these various "isms" are not merely "secondary contradictions" which influence and complicate the economic "primary contradiction". Rather, these various social relationships are absolutely vital to the structure and reproduction of bourgeois society, as much as (at times even more so than) the economic relationships. Bourgeois capitalism is thus a dragon with many heads—a hydra. Cut off one head and another grows in its place. To kill the beast, all of its heads must be attacked and killed at once. The tactics of the Leninists are entirely unsuited for this task. By focusing on the economic struggle between workers and capitalists, traditional Leninists limit their actions to labor unions, worker's parties, strikes, etc., and pay attention to other struggles—anti-sexist, anti-racist, etc. —only insofar as they provide advantages to the workers in their economic struggles.

From this point of view, the struggle against sexism is only important because it allows Leninists to point out that women are "super-exploited" or "doubly-exploited" as workers. To struggle against sexism itself is, in the traditional view, a distraction from the "real fight", that between labor and capital. The Leninists, in effect, try to utilize the other struggles in an effort to "distract" some of the hydra's heads, while they go about the business of killing what they perceive to be the "primary" one.

If the capitalist beast is to be killed, however, it must be attacked simultaneously on all fronts by a concerted, multi-faceted revolutionary organization. All of the various social dissident movements—feminists, anarchists, anti-racists, gay activists, socialists—must grow together to form a movement with complementary goals.

This process is aided by the fact that each of these movements in the course of its struggles finds that it is facing the same enemy as the others. Socialists find that those who benefit most from the capitalist system are those who own capital, and that capital-owners tend to be white males in positions of authority. Feminists find that the men who benefit most from sexism tend to be white property owners in positions of authority. Anarchists find that those who wield the most power and authority tend to be white male capital-owners, and anti-racists find that the most privileged whites are those who are male, wealthy and in positions of authority.

Thus, although each head of the capitalist hydra appears to be separate and independent, in reality they are all different faces of the same beast. To be defeated, bourgeois society must be attacked at all of its supporting structures. Failure to do this has been a major reason why radical movements have failed to produce any real revolutionary challenges to the existing social order. In the 1910's and 1930's, economic struggles on the part of the labor unions produced conditions that were at the least insurrectionary, but there were no complementary anti-racist, anti-sexist or anti-authoritarian components, and capitalism was able to isolate and overcome the threat. In the 1960's, radical feminist, anarchist, anti-racist and gay liberation movements were born, but they failed to coordinate their actions and were not supported by a militant workers' movement. Once again, capitalism was able to survive the challenge (though not without some battle damage).

The success of the bourgeoisie's power, then, is not simply that it controls the use of capital and thus controls the economy. One must be forced to ask why the workers accept and work within these obviously lopsided and exploitative economic conditions. Nobody holds a gun to the workers' heads and forces them to work for the capitalists. Except in the most rare and extreme circumstances, naked force and repression are hardly used at all by the monopolists. If the bourgeois mode of production is a dictatorship, it certainly appears to be a benevolent one.

The study of these non-economic social relationships explains how the capitalist system is able to maintain itself without resorting to physical coercion. The non-economic social relationships, between man and woman, between white and non-white, between boss and servant, between straight and gay—all serve to condition people to accept the bourgeois order of things as a natural, inevitable and inescapable part of reality. Every citizen of a capitalist country is born into a family unit, in which some members of the family are dependent on the income received by others. If one is to fulfill one's family role, one must of necessity participate in the capitalist wage system. Entry in the wage system is in turn conditioned by education, which is itself subjected to the limits of income, race and sexual roles.

In other words, the social relationships of the bourgeois order, taken as a whole, form a vast net of complex interactions which reinforce and reproduce each other, and serve to define, protect and propagate the physical, social and ideological conditions of bourgeois society. Bourgeois society thus produces a social, ideological and physical hegemony, a framework within which it can reproduce the conditions necessary for its own existence while at the same time excluding the necessary preconditions for a challenge to itself. No one forces the workers to labor in the factory, but the social and cultural hegemony of capitalism makes participation in the wage system a practical necessity. One must have a wage job in order to obtain one's necessaries of life, in order to play a family role, in order to participate in the educational system, and in order to perform a myriad of other social relationships.

In order to overthrow this array of hegemonic relationships, revolutionaries must attack each of these economic and non-economic structures and undermine them. More importantly, they must work to build an entirely new set of social relationships which can provide an alternative social reality, a new mode of production. In other words, revolutionaries can only win if they succeed in undermining bourgeois hegemony and in forming a new hegemony of their own.

Bourgeois hegemony can only be replaced by a socialist viewpoint; not merely socialist in the sense that the economic process must be controlled socially rather than by individual owners, but "socialist" in the sense that it is the conscious desire and activity of all members of human society and that it involves societal direction of all processes of production and propagation, including the economic, sexual, national and authoritarian spheres. The entire process of humanity's interaction with itself and its natural surroundings must be consciously and willfully directed by the totality of that society. It must be *social*-ist.

CONCLUSION

In his voluminous writings, Marx rarely made any reference to the process of transition between capitalism and socialism, or to the kinds of social relationships which would exist within the socialist mode of production. This is understandable, since Marx was not a Utopian, but preferred to deal with concrete reality rather than idealistic speculation or supposition. Since socialism did not yet exist, Marx was quite unable to describe its workings or mechanisms.

Today, despite the claims of the "Marxist-Leninists" and the "Communists", socialism still does not exist. As a result, we are equally unable to give an empirical description of what socialism looks like. Nevertheless, it is tempting to conclude our analysis of capitalism with a tentative look at its successor.

In order to do this, we must look again at the internal forces within the capitalist system which are steadily undermining it, as well as the actions being taken to prevent this process. The socialist system will spring from the internal crises of capitalism, just as capitalism itself resulted from the internal stresses which destroyed feudalism.

There are a number of trends visible within capitalism which point to its impending dissolution. In the processes of change and alteration which capitalism has undergone since the days of "laissez-faire economics", we can see the inability of capitalism to deal with the social and economic tasks which presently face it, and we can detect the beginnings of a new social and economic system which will be better suited to these new conditions.

The first of these changes to occur was the establishment of the joint stock corporation. In forming these conglomerates of capital, the capitalist class was acknowledging that the prior framework of private individual ownership of property was no longer suited to social circumstances, and that expanded production required the cooperation of a number of capital-owners under a joint management.

Today, this process has reached an extreme. Although the corporate sector of the economy is owned jointly by the capital-owning class (the small number of stockholders), it cannot be said that any corporation is "owned" by any individual (unless, of course, the corporation is itself a family-owned business). In essence, the capitalist system itself has done away with private property ownership and has introduced social property in its place.

In the heyday of the capitalist system, economic decisions were the prerogative of a single owner, who made his decisions individually and in his own short-term interests. Today, however, this capitalist ideal no longer applies. In the modern corporation, the search for long-term stability and profitability forces the corporations to make long-term plans for the investment and use of their capital and resources. These decisions are no longer made by individual property-owners; they are made by a network of hired managers and professionals. In essence, private short term investment has given way to joint long-term planning for the optimum utilization of resources.

Another crucial factor which resulted from the joint stock company is the separation (both legally and in practice) of ownership from management. In the early days of capitalism, the capital-owner had to serve as his own entrepreneur and manager. He could profit from his investment only if he himself made the decisions upon which profitability was based. This allowed the capitalist to justify his appropriation of surplus value as "compensation" for his decision-making entrepreneural role.

Today, however, the socialized capital-owning class has no such connection to business decision-making. Instead, the capitalist stockholders are able to hire the services of a network of professional managers, decision-makers and innovators who perform this role for them Those who own a majority of stock in a corporation have no need of business sense or entrepreneural ability; they can merely hire others who have these abilities. The stockholder-capitalist makes his living without lifting a finger. He performs no labor, produces no commodity, and develops no new innovation. The only thing he does is allow the managers to use his capital and then cash the dividend checks they send to him. Even if one accepts the argument that the capitalist as decision-maker receives his profits as compensation for his decision-making ability, one can certainly not make this argument when the capital-owner makes no decisions at all, but merely hires others to do this for him.

Thus, capitalist practice itself demonstrates that the capital-owner, the stockholder, is superfluous and parasitical. If the managers perform their tasks on behalf of the absentee stockholders, they can perform them just as well if those stockholders are deposed and replaced by elected representatives from the workplace and the surrounding community. There is no reason why the managers cannot be made responsible to the social entity as a whole rather than to the minority of stock-owners.

Developing methods of capitalist management are beginning to acknowledge this fact. In the days of individual capitalism, economic enterprises were essentially top-down affairs, mere extensions of a single capitalist who ran the enterprise in essentially dictatorial fashion—Carnegie Steel, Ford Motor Company, the Gould railway empire.

As corporations moved towards social ownership and control by professional managers, however, they turned from a vertical system of organization to a horizontal association of diverse economic enterprises. This process accelerated with the onset of the overproduction crisis, which forced corporations to diversify in order to survive.

The old "dictatorial" method of management works fine for a vertical organization which only had to monitor a small number of routine tasks, but top-down management fails miserably when faced with the task of integrating and coordinating a large number of diverse units.

As a result, modern managers have been forced to adopt methods which are more horizontal and "democratic", through the use of such concepts as project teams, work councils, ad hoc committees, and autonomous project teams. And, since this diverse economic process is too large and too involved to be overseen by a small number of hired managers, it has become necessary to integrate the workers in the shop more fully into this coordination process. This management concept was pioneered by the Japanese, and has since been adopted by US corporations, which have referred to it as "job enhancement" or "industrial democracy".

The long-term effects on the capitalist mode of production will be profound. These new management styles weaken the very core of the capitalist's *raison d'etre*. If management and workers can make economic decisions without the input of the owners, it is obvious that the owners are not needed and can be dispensed with. Furthermore, the increasing integration of workers into this management process will make the workers able to carry out these management tasks by themselves, thus making the professional management sector equally unnecessary. The capitalist program of "industrial democracy" is the beginning of a new social and economic structure which will eventually bring full control of the economy to the workers who run it. These infant "workers councils" represent the future society of worker control; they represent the beginnings of socialism.

Current political changes in the capitalist countries are hastening this process and adding to the framework within which the workers can seize control. As we have seen, many capitalist nations have nationalized key industries and placed them under direct state management, in order to protect the framework of the capitalist system. In this manner, a part of industry has been placed, if only theoretically, under the control of society as a whole rather than under the control of private owners.

New political movements make this process a future instrument of working class power. State ownership over industry means nothing to the working class unless it has ownership over the state, and right now the bourgeois state is completely dominated by the moneyed interests. However, this domination is also beginning to fall apart.

In the early republics, the right to vote was granted only to white male property-owners. Since then, working class struggle has forced expansion of the right to vote, and today suffrage is almost universal.

This is still a hollow right, however, since the moneyed interests completely dominate the campaign and electoral process, and thus limit the options from which the voters can choose. Current movement towards public campaign financing and legal limits on the terms of elected officials, however, will weaken the grip of the wealthy elites on the election process, and the increasing empowerment of the referendum and initiative will place more and more political power in the hands of the working class.

The most significant step which has been taken in this direction is the legal addition of local community and working class representatives to corporate decision-making boards. Laws such as the German "co-determination law" and regulations in the US which limit the actions of corporate plant closings show the beginnings of a trend towards joint economic decisions made by community representatives and worker representatives, and thus represent the beginnings of a new social structure which will allocate economic resources without the need for capitalist property-owners or their professional managers. The economic and political decisions of a social group will be the prerogative of that social group. Economic decisions will be made, not according to the criteria of wealth and profit, but according to that of the production of things that are needed and the efficient distribution of these things. Production and distribution will follow the formula, "From each according to ability, to each according to need."

The high productivity of the capitalist system is the final method by which it is undermining itself. Given the incredible productive forces that could result from the full utilization of productive capacity, it will be possible for an industrialized society to produce all of its needs while utilizing only one-half or one-third of its present work force. Farming has already undergone such an explosion of productivity under capitalism. While under feudalism nearly all of the population was engaged in production of food, under capitalism the impact of machinery has produced a society where more than enough food can be produced using only 5% of the population.

Similarly, manufacturing ability has expanded to the point where most people simply do not need to produce anything. The capitalists recognize this fact by acknowledging that acceptable levels of unemployment have been rising steadily over the past few decades. In addition, the capitalist process of industrialization and mechanization has introduced a means of reducing the working population still further, by replacing the human worker with machinery, automation and robotic factories.

Capitalism is thus caught in a contradiction which it cannot escape. In order for people to obtain the necessaries of life, they must have income from jobs, but the capitalist process itself is steadily eroding and eliminating these jobs. Thus, capitalism cannot meet the needs of the social body, and must be altered. It must be forced to develop methods of distribution which are not based on the income from wage labor. Rather than distributing scarce commodities on the basis of who has the money to pay for them, capitalism is now faced with the problem of distributing abundant resources according to who needs them.

The result is a social system of production and distribution which is not based on profit, wage labor or capital accumulation, but on the production and distribution of useful things; on the production of use-values, not exchange values. It is a *social*-ist system, in which human needs determine what is done, not the desires of private property-owners. It is a society which is characterized by social control over resources rather than private, by long-term planning rather than short-term profit, by the integration of political and economic decisions rather than the separation of them, and by production for use rather than production for profit.

Such a socialist system will also free us to develop the full potential of our human interactions and relationships. Free from the constraining limits imposed by the bourgeois need to replicate and propagate existing social relationships through sexism, racism, heterosexism, authoritarianism, etc., humans will be free to interact with each other in any way they desire.

The full process of social interaction, between humans and nature, between man and woman, between worker and non-worker, between straight and gay, between order-giver and order-taker, will be under the direct and conscious control of human needs and desires, by human beings who are fully conscious of their existence as social beings. Human needs and desires will once again be the root of human actions, and humans will once again become *Homo sapiens*, "conscious humans".

Lightning Source UK Ltd.
Milton Keynes UK
29 November 2010

163612UK00009B/196/A